Your Patient Attraction Secret Weapon

How to Have a Referral-Driven Dental Practice and Never Advertise Again

Ron Sheetz

Printed in the United States of America

ISBN: 1505759676
ISBN-13: 978-1505759679

RJ Media Magic, Inc.
2824 Burden Rd.
Cleveland, OH 44134
(440) 606-6244

DEDICATION

I dedicate this book to my wife Anne, whose relentless support over the past 20+ years who has been my foundation (my rock). To my son Brandon who is the most gentle and warm hearted soul, who inspires me to be better. To my daughter Olivia in whom I see a lot of myself. And finally, to my mom, who provided the words so many years ago that set me on my path at a time when she was at her own personal cross road in life

What Dental Professionals Internationally Say About Ron Sheetz

"Network quality video testimonials are a no-brainer for practices that want to obtain category killer advantages in their niche and location. I've seen far too many "high-end" productions vended to dentists that fall flat on results and quality especially when compared to the expertise Ron brings to the table for obtaining the stories from your patients that really matter. The testimonials he shot for us years ago are still working to bring us new clients."

Dr. James McAnally (Dentistry's #1 ethical sales training @ CaseAcceptance.com)

"A HUGE "thanks" for making my last event a major success. Your skills and easy-going nature immediately put my members at ease. They provided truthful, from the heart thoughts about what we do for them and the value they get from it. In short, your work speaks for itself.
I've gotten testimonials on my own, but they were nowhere near this effective.
In fact, something most don't know: An ineffective testimonial can actually HURT a sale. Yes, if someone goes about this wrong (and I've seen it), an improperly done testimonial can kill sales. Every time a new customer shows up, I'm reminded and thankful for the hard work and effort you put in. What's more, you make doing business with you incredibly easy. And, I can't tell you how much that means to a guy like me who's got a number of business interests to tend to."

Jerry Jones (JerryJonesDirect.com & DentalConfidential.com)

"Your expertise in creating a documentary of my practice, along with many patient testimonials, has given me a powerful tool to use in my marketing. Just one application for it, in our local cinema, on the big screen, so new patients keep streaming in thanks to the loop we created from your professionally done film. I can't thank you enough for the splendid work and for helping us to attract a wealth of new patients!"

Dr. Pauline Demetrakopulos – StHelenaDentist.com

"Ron truly earns the logo, "Video Marketing Guru". Video testimonials are perhaps the most powerful method to sway potential patients to the practice and Ron has a bullet proof technique for getting patients to happily give powerful testimonials, right on the spot. If you are looking to direct the growth of your practice in this new age, you should include Ron's technique in your armamentarium."

Dr. David Pearce – BaldwinsvilleGentleDentist.com

"Ron was able to capture and communicate the culture of our practice in a unique documentary film by interviewing Tim and I, our staff and many of our patients. We now have a marketing tool that gives a new patient a clear understanding of what it's like to be a patient in our practice before they ever visit or call us. His unique documentary has given us a way to really differentiate our practice from the other offices in the area. Also, we recently bought a second practice and we mailed a DVD of our film to all the patients in the practice to introduce ourselves to them in a unique and very personal way. The patients were able to "meet" us before they even walked in our door. Additionally, we've been able to apply different parts of the film strategically on our website. Ron really knows how to market a dental practice in a unique and effective way."

Margaret A. Valega, DDS & D. Timothy Pike, DDS

"It was like talking to you and no one sensed that camera was there after about 30-seconds. I see a lot of videos on the Internet, but I don't see any good dental ones. You were the right person at the right time to come along and I knew I had to jump on it."

Dr. Gary Newell – NewellClarkson.com

"You were right, when you have the right person asking the right questions you forget about the video camera and you can have a natural conversation. I felt very comfortable talking to you and the questions you asked were everyday experiences."

Dr. John Francis – PerioDrs.com

It's easy to talk to people, talking to the camera is more difficult. The conversation approach is really helpful. You're very good at guiding the conversation with your goal in mind as a marketer. How to take the really important pieces and apply them where they will have the greatest effectiveness. That's an art in itself.

Dr. Rudy Wassenaar – WilliamsLakeSmiles.ca

I think you were just great. If they weren't getting where you wanted you had a very natural way of making them understand and you were able to ask the right questions to get back on track where you wanted to go. If I had to do it myself, or rely on my team to do it, it would never get done. Unfortunately I get caught up in the everyday operations of the office, but the bigger point I'd add is the fear, the fear of failing. I don't like to fail so doing something new brings the risk of failing, so it can hold me back. I needed to commit to it. The only reason I had you do it is because I knew it would get done and it would be great.

Dr. Yvan Tesolin – MonCentreDentaire.com

"It's nice to not have to repeat the same message 10,000 times when it can be recorded and it can be seen over and over."

Dr. Michael Saso – DrSaso.com

Ron know just about everything there is to acquiring and using testimonials in your practice.

Dr. Jeff Anzalone – AnzalonePeriodontics.com

YOU DON'T HAVE TO READ THIS BOOK TO GET HIGHLY PERSUASIVE TESTIMONIALS OR ONLINE REVIEWS FOR YOUR DENTAL PRACTICE RIGHT NOW

I understand getting testimonials from your patients, especially on video is a pain in the butt. If you're like most dentists with whom I've worked, you've probably tried everything under the sun to get it done, even paying your staff to get them captured, but to no avail.

If it's been a problem for you and you want to short-cut the whole process and get it done; finally have patient testimonials that will work to attract the right kind of patient to your practice and put a system in place for capturing them and getting them implemented into your practice marketing immediately then go to page 154 for your 'Fast Track to Patient Testimonials and Perfect Online Reviews'.

CONTENTS

Preface

What If What You Knew About Patient Testimonials Was Wrong?

Jerry A. Jones, *founder* | JerryJonesDirect.com

You have to really look at the psychology of the average patient or prospective patients. From my experience in and around Dentistry, I've discovered there are really only two reasons why the majority of Americans avoid the Dentist, and why it's very convenient for them to avoid the dentist. These two excuses are also most easily "bought into" by peers, friends, family and yes, even Dentists. In other words, the excuses are very easy to believe. It's *usually* B.S.

The two excuses are pain and money. If you truly analyze all the reasons patients will give you for avoiding the Dentist or avoiding accepting treatment once they do get there, they all boil down to pain and money. Patients don't want to be in pain by going to the Dentist; psychological, emotional or physical. What they don't realize is that you, the Dentist, is there to get them out of pain and to help them avoid it. But they're afraid; so they use pain as an excuse. The human response to the *fear of* pain is avoidance. And because so many patients choose to avoid their fear, to push through what makes them so uncomfortable, too many miss out on the real benefits of Dentistry.

To the surprise of many Dental practitioners, skill and experience are not what will ultimately get a patient past their fear and agree to your case presentation. As a true professional, and in accordance with the oath you took, you owe it to your patients and all the people out there who are not yet your patient, to do everything within your power to get them to accept the cases you present. Not just to make more money; but, to provide more patients the benefits of your skill and experience. You can't be a problem solver, a professional who changes people's lives, if you can't influence people to be your patient.

So, fear is at the top of many patients' list and you have to stop accepting this as an excuse.

The second B.S. excuse is money, or the lack of it, for treatment. In our current economy, and at the risk of sounding like some other blithering idiot on TV, our economy is rough, still, in many areas. There's no question. People are having a tougher go of it. Now, does that mean that your dental office should slump as a result? No. You may have to see more people to get the same numbers. It's a math game. If you're not closing the same number of cases or treatment plans that you were on ten patients – if you were closing nine out of ten before but now you're only closing six, you have to see 15 patients to get back to the same ratio, or to keep the same numbers going that you had before.

If you really boil the money excuse down, it too is about fear; fear of the departure of their money.

So money and fear keep people from seeking you out. How then can you address these 'elephants in the room' in your marketing pieces, and how do you get them to pick up the telephone and call you?

Unlike other businesses you have the added challenge of convincing people to call. If you were a dry cleaner, they wouldn't be afraid of calling from an ad, but your obstacle is bigger; getting patients to call the practice is the heavy lifting your marketing really has to carry. You can't call them. You don't know who is in pain or who needs to be at the Dentist or who's considering going to a Dentist. You just can't go to the yellow pages and start dialing.

Getting patients to pick up the phone is a huge challenge. You can send out direct mail pieces, you can run ads in the newspapers, you can position yourself online to be someone that is sought after and ultimately called.

To do that you have to remove the barriers of fear and money. Barriers are most easily removed by having convincing sales copy, by proof, evidence, by pictures, and things like patient testimonials. Fortunately you have the ability to use patient testimonials in your advertisements and marketing. My other client base, financial advisors, cannot use testimonials. There are stiff governmental regulations preventing the use of this powerful form of social proof by financial professionals; but not you. Are you using them? Are you using them correctly?

Next, you're tasked with creating all the proof yours is the right place to call. You're the doctor they should trust. And here are the '18 reasons why.' And don't worry if you're scared; don't worry if you have had bad experiences or bad memories, because here are the 21 ways we alleviate all that stuff. We're going to pamper you and not belittle you because you haven't been to the dentist in 37 years.

You have to provide all this proof that they're making the right decision to call. But they're afraid and they may not know you're "someone" that can really identify with them on a personal level.

You're a doctor and patients view you as a figure of authority. It's human conditioning. We're conditioned from a young age to respect and revere our elders and those in positions of power and authority. From childhood we're told that a doctor is someone important. We need to listen because they have good advice.

This is both an advantage and an obstacle because despite the reverence people have for you, they cannot identify with you as a 'real' person. It's up to you to change that. You have to bring yourself down to a level that commands respect, yet shows or exhibits that you're real, reachable, approachable, and, you're someone they can have a conversation with, a relationship with and not feel intimidated by and not feel disempowered.

Despite what business you might think you're in, you're ultimately in the relationship business. The doctors in my office, Wellness Springs Dental® of Salem, (www.WellnessSpringsDental.com) work first on connecting with and building personal rapport with patients before they ever get around to discussing dentistry or treatment plans. For us, it goes a long way in creating a relationship. And dialogue is important. Dialogue means "two." You've got two people in a dialogue. Doctors who have a difficult time closing treatment operate on monologues. And, they generally speak above the understanding of their patients, instead of at a very basic 6th grade level of communication.

In other words the Doc talks and when they're done talking, the patient goes, *"Oh, good Lord. What did he just say? I didn't understand a word he said. It sounds expensive. Get me out of here."*

The Doc that intellectually overwhelms and intimidates gets nowhere.

And so creating an experience for the patient pre-visit or during the visit that shows, *"Hey, our doctors here are real, they're reachable, and you can have a dialogue with them. You can talk to them and they'll listen to you. You can explain to them why you're where you're at in your oral healthcare, and they're not going to make you feel guilty about past decisions."* Guilt is a powerful trigger, it creates fear, resentment and embarrassment and ultimately accomplishes nothing.

It's also imperative to show yourself at a level where others can see you as a real person, just like them. It's just that Dentistry is what you do for a living. Show your family life and a little bit about your office, your employees, hobbies, etc.

A lot of the Docs I work with… one of the things so many overlook and is the easiest and most direct path for getting patients to connect with them, and still respect the authority, is through their patients; the existing patients they have.

You see, each of your patients have stories; stories of pain and fear and money concerns. It's what existing patients share with your prospective patients and when the prospective patients become your patient, they'll share the benefits and experience you provide. This is a transfer of trust. If that patient, the one speaking to me, is like me, and you (the Dentist) helped them and they trusted you, then you can help me and I can trust you; it's a variation on *'any friend of yours is a friend of mine.'*

Patient testimonials connect the dots unlike anything you can say or publish. It's authentic. You can't fake it. It removes all doubt from the equation. When you have social proof and you have others talking about you on your behalf, it removes doubt.

When Mary's talking about how she was frustrated with her dentures, and thank goodness Dr. Jones was able to fix her dentures in place with a couple of implants, and it was painless and it was nothing like she had made it up to be in her mind, and it was easy, and, "I'm so thrilled with Dr. Jones." Hearing and seeing that from Mary herself, who is representative of the prospective patient, who's in their socioeconomic, their geographic area, within their demographic makeup, culture, all of these are hugely impactful.

Because, Mary, who is also a 58-year-old woman, is watching this lady on video talk about her dentures and how she was frustrated. And Mary sits there with dentures clicking around in her mouth, getting more frustrated by the minute thinking, *"Why am I continuing to deal with this? I'm 58, I deserve to have what she has. I've paid my dues, dang it. I want what she has."*

This has little to do with the doctor. It has everything to do with two people having a conversation of sorts, as if they were two 58-year old ladies sitting at lunch one sharing her experience with the other. Some might call this a referral, though in this dialogue it's testimony; one person talking, sharing, emoting and the other listening, watching and feeling.

Anything the doctor says about him or herself in advertisements and marketing really run off a prospective patient like water off a duck's back. When I see it used in marketing this way it's nothing more than ego, *ad nauseam* to a prospective patient. What one patient can say about you in a few minutes is far more powerful than anything the doc could possibly say about themselves in 50 hours of video or a single ad.

As a matter of fact, I've never run an ad for my dental office here in Salem that has ever included any sort of accolade for or about the doctor. Never have I ever sent out a postcard or a direct mail piece or a newspaper ad or anything like that which brags about how great our doctors are, or how wonderful our doctors are. Or having a doctor talk about the institutes they've attended, or the thousands of hours of continuing education they have. Because the bottom line is, it doesn't matter to the patient. And why would you put something in front of the patient that may repel them or come across as braggadocios?

The bigger issue at play here is what <u>isn't</u> said; it's what's going through the prospective patient's mind, the outcome, that perfect smile they've always dreamt of, the benefits you and only you can provide them. Psychologists call this *future pacing*; a prospective patient internalizing and emotionally identifying with the results you can provide. This is the most powerful emotion you can unleash within a prospective patient and you're able to influence them without having to 'sell' them...because I know how much Docs hate to sell cases. This power of influence is something you can't replicate in any other format. You can't get that from good or great ad copy alone. Testimonials fill this void, if you will, that can't be touched with anything else. People will self identify and pursue what they want and the money will never stand in the way of what they really want. We're hard-wired this way. Testimonials remove the pain and fear excuses.

I can tell you the financial services industry is far worse off not being able to use testimonials. You can and you should. This is a powerful tool. Every human wants the ability to smile. Everybody wants to be happy. We don't wake up wanting to be grumpy or upset or having a bad day. We all want to be happy. We're born with it.

If you have patients who have been with you for years, generations of family members who keep coming back and patients who refer others, then you have the ability to show and exhibit trust through testimonials. The ability to transmit trust, the transference of authority and the transference of trust that takes place in a video testimonial environment, cannot be replicated in another environment, unless the two people were dialoging in person, face-to-face. Video testimonials are the medium through which you can demonstrate you're worthy of their trust. It's completely genuine.

There's a specific talent and skill required to be able to extract what folks have experienced and what they feel, and then capture that on video and audio. Most patients can't enunciate it without being led by someone that is trained and understands how to elicit those emotions from them. Your team should be trained to get that process going… to elicit testimonials from patients, to plant the idea and create the culture within your office.

I'm sure that's why you're reading this particular book at this particular time; you're ready. You've wrestled with it for long enough. It's been a thorn in your side. It's like the splinter that's gotten under your fingernail and you just can't get it out. It pains you to think about it any longer. You're at your wits end. You've told your team you want patient testimonials, more patient testimonials, better quality patient testimonials, but no matter how emphatic you are or how much you talk about it, nothing gets done.

If over half the population doesn't go to a dentist now because of fear or money or whatever BS reason they tell themselves, it's your duty, no, *your obligation* to be the authority, the influencer, the problem solver and the changer of peoples' lives they want you to be. They need you to be.

Testimonials are the sharing of an emotional experience that show others cutting through their fear, cutting through their trepidation, cutting through their apprehension about going to the Dentist. This is where the real secret in case acceptance lies.

I've worked with Ron, I've seen him in action and in this book he reveals his secrets. He pulls back the curtain on all of his techniques, strategies and scripts, the tools for which his private clients pay him handsomely. If you can utilize what Ron does (and gives you here) to penetrate just a small, tiny fraction of that 50 percent that doesn't go to a Dentist, you're going to become wildly busy and wealthy.

If you want the ultimate differentiator between your practice and somebody else's, you will employ every system Ron shares with you in this book.

Booker T. Washington said, *"Success always leaves footprints."* If you follow the footprints Ron has left for you in the area of getting and applying patient testimonials, then it will take everything you're doing now in your practice and take it to a level that is just unmatched. It's unreplicatable. It will put you in a category of one. And in order to be successful in any business, you have to stand out. You have to attract attention. You have to attract interest. You have to have people desire to do business with you and Ron's system will give you that. I've seen what other companies do. I've seen them attempt to do what Ron does, and frankly, there's nobody that even comes close.

By the time you finish this book you'll have the knowledge and tools to be able to finally capture great patient testimonials in your practice as well as tactical strategies for implementing them into your marketing and advertising. You'll also have access to the tools for both automating the entire process of getting the highest caliber testimonials on a consistent basis with virtually no intervention by you or your team.

When I read books such as this I highlight sentences and paragraphs, dog-ear corners and make notes in the margin in order to make the book a more specific resource for my business and me. I encourage you to do the same.

About Jerry... Jerry A. Jones is the CEO of Jerry Jones Direct (JJD), an over two-decade old marketing and advertising firm whose clients include Dentists and Financial Services Advisors in the US, Canada, Australia and England. He's a widely-published author of several books and thought leader, writing opinion papers and articles for a variety of publications. Jerry also publishes five different newsletters and two magazines every month, leads dental mastermind sessions, and creates marketing and advertising campaigns for his private client Financia l Advisors, Dentists and ClearPath Society® Members. He is also the Founder & CEO of Wellness Springs Dental® in Salem, Oregon, which includes an incredible group of four Doctors and an amazing team. Wellness Springs Dental® will be offering national dental office franchises in 2014. Info @ www.WellnessSpringsDental.com. More information on Jerry can be found at www.JerryJonesDirect.com, for Clear Path Society go to https://tg133.isrefer.com/go/CPsilver/ronsheetz/ or my monthly Dental Confidential newsletter go to www.DentistryConfidential.net.

CHAPTER #1

I PUT MY MONEY WHERE MY MOUTH IS

In October of 2003 I thought life was good. I was 38 and I had worked for the same man, my mentor, for 23 years and I was in control of my future, or so I thought. In a moment's time it all changed. Bob Keith, my mentor and surrogate father, the man who'd taken me under his wing and taught me everything I knew about business and entrepreneurship, fell victim to a devastating stroke. It rendered him partially paralyzed on his right side, and he was no longer able to run the business he'd grown and I had so much latitude in. Unbeknownst to me, the business wasn't doing as well as we were led to believe, despite the 5-figure a month sales I was bringing in at the time. My first operational activity was to find that the company was behind in federal payroll taxes.

On December 21, 2003, only 4 days before Christmas I laid off the entire staff of the independent video production company I'd come to think would be mine. It was too far gone to revive. On January 31, 2004 Bob's wife and I officially closed the doors on A-Video Lease and Production, Inc.

Contemplating what to do now, considering I was recently married, a new homeowner with a first-time mortgage and expecting our first child, I was perplexed. I told my wife I wasn't sure what to do. What she said put everything into perspective. She said, "You'll do what you do." On February 1, 2004, 24-hours after closing one door I opened another and founded RJ Media Magic, Inc. I started my own company and for the first time, my future was truly in my hands.

I began leveraging every business relationship I'd developed over my previous 21 years. I did some repeat business with clients bringing them over to my company. Several of those clients are still with me today.

The Cold Call That Changed Everything For Me

2 months after starting RJMM I received a call from a new prospect. Debbie Short called our A-Video Lease yellow pages ad. I received the call because I'd kept AVL's phone number active and had calls forwarded to my new number. I'll never forget the call. It came in at 9:07am on a Tuesday morning. I answered the call in my usual manner and on the other end I heard, *"Do you make videos?"* It wasn't a pleasant voice, it was one of aggravation (you can read Debbie's story in her own words at the end of this chapter). During the diagnostic meeting, one of the first observations I made was that they had no client testimonials in any of the marketing. When I pointed it out, Don Meuser, the owner, blurted in a similar tone as Debbie's when she'd first called me (frustrated), *"We've tried to get them and can't!"* I was young, naive and full of ambition to make my new company successful and capitalize on my first new prospect. In response to Don I replied, "Give me a list of your top 20 clients and I'll get them." He called me on it and before I walked out of his office, I had the list of his 20 top clients, and absolutely no system for getting them as video testimonials. It wasn't the first time I'd committed to a promise and to that point, I'd never failed to deliver on my promises and I wasn't about to start here.

I went to work on creating a system and put it to the test immediately on Don's project. Long story short, I scheduled and interviewed, on video, 19 of the 20 clients on the list. The one I didn't get gave me the BS story they couldn't give a testimonial because it was against corporate policy to endorse any one vendor.

I spent the next 5 years improving my system and in 2007 I applied it to marketing work I was hired by my family dentist (Dr. Manbir Pannu) to do for her practice. To her, as with Don Meuser, I suggested she needed patient testimonials and she said, "We've tried to get them." Now I had the opportunity to test my system in dentistry… and it worked, again, just as it had the first time with

Cleveland Door Controls. In 2009 I connected with Dr. James McAnally who invited me to speak at his dental marketing summit in Orlando, Florida. I spoke on video marketing and only touched on patient testimonials, but it was testimonials that generated the most questions and conversation from attendees. As an opportunist and entrepreneur, I quickly put together a program for the docs and offered it to them. Again, another opportunity to prove my system under fire… and it worked without flaw. I've spent the last 6 years continuing to apply my system in dental practices across North America and I now have dentists following my articles and newsletters in Canada, England, Australia and Taiwan. The material I will share with you in this book is a sum of my system and experience applying it in independent practices across the country.

Debbie Short tells of her first call to Ron and working with him

"The president of our company had, what I thought was, a simple request to produce a virtual video tour of our company. We wanted to give prospective clients a brief, yet concise, overview of our company; something 5 to 7 minutes long that we could put on our website. Little did I know that something this simple could be perceived by so many as being challenging, time consuming and ridiculously expensive. But after literally 8-hours (I lost count of how many I talked to) on the telephone with production companies and agencies in Cleveland and Chicago I was quoted from $10,000 to $25,000 to produce such a video (and those were the ones at which I was able to reach anyone by phone, others either failed to answer or never called back). It seemed each organization I talked with was quick to quote me a price, yet hardly anyone probed to ask the details behind my inquiry. The few that did only asked half heartedly, "What do you want" and "How long do you want it to be?" I got the general feeling my call was interrupting something apparently valuable of their attention. It boggled my mind that I could be quoted such unreasonable costs when they had virtually no details on the specifics of our demands, nor any interest to find out.

Even though it seemed like a futile exercise I made one more call to RJ Media Magic and out of sheer frustration and aggravation I blurted out, "DO YOU MAKE VIDEOS?" to the pleasant hello I received from the other end of the phone. After a moment of silence, Ron Sheetz calmly stated, "Yes", and, accurately reading the frustration in my voice he continued by asking, "what would you like to accomplish with your video?" Within in minutes Ron asked additional questions that were targeted at understanding our company, our clientele, and our ultimate objectives. Unlike others who's interest seemed only to "make a video", I felt Ron was truly interested in helping us meet our needs. He also was successful at lowering my blood pressure!

Per my request, he did quote me an investment range for the project based on my descriptions, though suggested we meet to further understand our complete needs and determine if he could help or not. I completely respected his direct approach and candor, as has

Don our President and owner.

Ron Sheetz ultimately produced our virtual company tour (which can be seen at www.clevelanddoorinc.com) on budget and on time; and most importantly, effectively differentiates us from our competitors. His consistent and unwavering passion, and "can do attitude" has made Ron a trusted source to Cleveland Door Controls. We recently celebrated our 50th Anniversary in business and he is updating our virtual tour. Ron knows his stuff. He's done his homework, learning our company's strengths and what makes us different from competitors. He is a magician at crafting just the right message for us to maximize its effectiveness."

This is not a dentist however it represents how I approach every client's project.

Ron Sheetz

Chapter 2

REASON WHY MARKETING

My grandfather was born on November 30, 1909. By the age of 19 he lived through the great American depression. He was old enough to know what it meant to be poor. He knew what it was like to make money, to try to buy bread and milk and what a hardship it was on his family of 10. He lived to be 100 and from the end of the depression until he passed away he lived everyday preparing for the next depression. Every financial decision he made was made with the idea that if he spent money on something and the second financial depression hit, how would he be able to support his family.

I had the pleasure of having my grandfather along with me a lot when I traveled to college campuses performing my comedy hypnosis show. We spent a lot of hours together in the car traveling and I heard his stories of his time on the railroad and of my family lineage. But I never fully understood why he and my grandmother lived the way they did until recently in preparing for this book. My grandparents lived a modest lifestyle. They didn't spend their money lavishly, quite the opposite. I recall opportunities when my grandparents had the chance to buy real estate as investment property, but didn't. They didn't because my grandfather was fearful the depression would hit again and he never wanted to experience the same financial hardship he had when he was 19 years old.

I tell this story because it's a powerful example of an origin story. He was a smart man, a hard worker and he and my grandmother could have made a lot more money, but his entire life was dictated by his early experience. If I would have known this story a lot earlier it would have helped me appreciate why he did what he did. His early experiences defined his values, his work ethic and the direction his life took. With a brief story, an explanation of where he came from everyone would have had a better understanding of who Otto Gualtier was. I finally figured it out, but most of my family never did. They knew who he was, but they never fully understood his values, who he was, and why he did what he did.

Batman, Crime Fighter or Freak?

Who are you and why do you do what you do? You have an origin story and you're probably not using it in your practice because you don't think it's important to how people perceive you as a dentist. The normal tendency in business is to separate your personal and professional lives, but people don't buy from businesses they buy from people; people they know, like, and trust. I've been in business for over 30 years and in that time I believed in keeping who I am personally separate from who I am professionally. As a professional magician and comedy hypnotist I knew how important it was to be myself on stage and how powerful it was in getting an audience to like me, yet in business I thought there was a need for the duality.

I first heard Dan Kennedy speak on the importance of using your origin story in your marketing in 2006. He uses the example of the comic book character Batman. Who is Batman and how did he become a caped crusading hero? Even if you don't follow the Batman comics or movies you surely know the origin story of Batman. As a young boy Bruce Wayne witnessed his parent's murder and from that moment forward he vowed to battle crime. That's the condensed version, but without knowing that story you would otherwise see Batman as a masked freak running around the city kicking the crap out of everyone. It's important for the audience to know his origin story, to have a connection with who he is and therefore understand why he does what he does. Every comic book hero has an origin story and it's told in some form in every episode of the story. Without it the audience has no frame of reference or connection with the character.

Your origin story helps your patients form an opinion about you; it defines who you are, why you do what you do, and it gives you credibility with your patients. In most cases it gives your potential patients a point of connection with you. Like the Batman character, your audience will have an appreciation for who you are. Today's dental patients are looking for a dentist they can develop a long term relationship with. When 75% of the population fears the dentist, or has some level of anxiety about seeing a dentist, the prospect of looking for a new dentist is not an activity the prospective patient looks forward to.

What Your Dental Patients Are Telling You

I've interviewed hundreds of dental patients and there are commonalities that I've concluded about the dentists they see based on how comfortable they feel with that dentist. Here are the conclusions I've drawn based on the work I've done interviewing those patients. This is not a scientifically concluded study, rather information I've gathered for the work I do with my dental clients. It is information I have extrapolated based on the real experiences as spoken by real patients. Keep in mind this is a simplification and summary of my findings, but it gives you a picture of what the patients who have not yet found your practice are feeling at a visceral level.

- The vast majority of dental patients (approximately 80%) have had either a bad or poor dental experience at some point in their life; as a child or young adult. This experience makes them hesitant to see a dentist. When they do reach a point in their life when they can't put off seeing a dentist any longer, the process of finding a dentist is painful because they're deathly afraid of reliving their past experiences. Like my grandfather being afraid of living through a depression again, the thoughts, actions and decisions of a dental patient are driven by their past experiences.

- However, when a patient finds a dentist they're comfortable with, they are extremely loyal to them and willing to sing their praises from the highest mountain top. One patient I interviewed, Shannon, had such a destructive experience with a dentist as a child that she will never get past the fear of the dentist, but she found one who helps her manage her anxiety. She told me she still feels anxious even when coming for a cleaning, but she's comforted by the fact that the dentist will help her get through it. It took a lot of trust building on his part to get her to that point. For Shannon, the trust was built on her comfort with the person first, and the education and technology second.

- Patients know a dentist must have a given level of education and technology to be a dentist…it's assumed. But, they have no way of knowing what the dentist's skill level is with that education and technology until they actually experience it. They don't know what happens behind the front door of your practice. They're basing their frame of reference as to what happens to patients in your practice on what they've experienced in other practices. As a marketer, you're battling a lot of negative emotions and experiences. For patients, perception IS reality. Regardless of how great you are as a clinician, patients will do everything they can to avoid reliving past painful experiences. That may not be true in your practice, but they're real to the patients, and your marketing materials are your frontline to belaying those perceptions. In marketing your services, you're battling all that negative baggage from a patient's first contact with a dental practice.

So, how do you get prospective patients to develop a feeling of personal connection and affinity with you, that will help them get past their fear of picking up the telephone to schedule a consultation with you? The easiest place to start is connecting with them through your origin story. Think about your relationship with your spouse. Early on when courting, what were your earliest conversations about? Did you talk about likes and dislikes, what your hobbies were, music, movies, etc? From those early conversations, each of you were trying to figure out who the other person was and whether or not there was a connection. This figuring out of other people is basic human nature, yet as businesses, the tendency is to put emphasis on promoting *what we do*, rather than *who we are*. The conclusion you can draw from my non-scientific study is that most dental patients are judging you as a person before they're ever judging you as a dentist. Unconsciously they're asking themselves *"do I like this person and can I trust him or her?"* You can have all the education, skill, and technology in the world, but if the patient can't get past their personal trust of you, the rest doesn't matter.

So what are people trying to figure out about you as a dentist? This comes from both my personal work with Dan Kennedy, his teachings of trust-based marketing and my own personal experiences with its application. In Dan's book, **No B.S. Trust-Based Marketing** (Amazon.com or NoBSBooks.com), he defines the *"Nine Gates to Customer Commitment."* His use of the term "Gates" is very appropriate. A gate is often locked and only the right key can open the gate. In getting to trust, Dan actually states there are 9 keys and most of, if not all 9, must be satisfied before a patient can get to a level of trust with you.

As he states in his book, the gates are;

1. Is this person "for real"? (Authenticity)
2. Are they telling me the truth? (Believability)
3. Are they knowledgeable and competent? (Credibility)
4. Is he or she appropriate for me? (Feasibility of relationship)
5. Is he or she listening or just "peddling"? (Customized solutions)
6. Overall, can he or she be relied on? (Safety)
7. Do I understand (enough about) what he or she is going to do for me? (Comfort)
8. Am I making the best choice vs. other choices? (Superiority)
9. Am I paying a fair price? (Value)

I have yet to meet a patient who actually has the above list written down and searches the Internet directories of dentists interviewing them to systematically check them off and get to the "right" dentist. I don't think this would ever happen, because most people haven't thought about what they want in a dentist, they'll just know it when they find it.

Before your potential patient can get to this unwritten checklist, they first have to connect with you.

Birds of a Feather Flock Together

In studying human nature, most of what we do and how we act, and how your patients make decisions are based on emotional, instinctive factors. I was trained in a time when sales tactics were very effective. Professional sales trainers are still teaching closing techniques, and I've learned them all, but they don't work as well today. Why? Because they're techniques used by salespeople, and your patients can spot a salesperson a mile away.

It takes a more subtle approach to "sell" a patient into your services. People don't want to be sold anything and in today's environment with the Internet they can shop without being pressured into buying something. On the other hand, people love to buy; and when they find what they want, they'll pay virtually any price for it. Yes, they'll pay any price for what they want.

Recently, Hostess, the manufacturer and distributor of snack foods like Twinkies, Ho-Ho's, and Wonder Bread announced they were shutting the company down after 82 years. Prior to their announcement, their most popular snack food, Twinkies, normally sold in grocery stores for about $2.99 a box. After the announcement, people were paying as much as $500.00 a box on Ebay. The product didn't change, but the supply for it was going away. An even bigger marketing lesson is people weren't buying Twinkies because they're a great snack cake, quite the contrary. People were buying a piece of their past. Amongst boomers, Twinkies were a common school lunch box favorite. My point is, people will pay for what they really want. You need to know what your patients want, and how much they're willing to pay to get it. This requires marketing based more on who you are, than what you do.

Even when you find out what they want, it still requires a certain amount of selling of your expertise and skill, but today it takes ethical selling. There are ways to sell ethically without coming across like a "salesperson".

In his Trust-Based marketing book, Dan Kennedy defines 26 specific trust triggers; precise elements that will elevate your communication and connection with prospective patients. Affinity tops the list and is the most effective. Yet in all the work I've been paid handsomely for by private clients, regardless of the industry, but especially amongst dentists; affinity is the element most will argue is insignificant with their patients and prospective patients, when in reality it's the most important.

People Will Buy <u>You</u>; BEFORE They Buy What You Sell

Bob Keith, my first mentor, taught me this and he was right. But how do you sell yourself? By being yourself! How do you be yourself, when you're trying to be their dentist? This is where affinity comes in and it's the easiest thing you can do. Share your loves, your likes, and your hobbies.

I have interviewed countless patients who say they chose their dentist based on where he or she was originally from, or from what college they hail. This is not the best basis on which to pick a dentist, but I have one dentist's patients who I've recorded and documented to say they picked the doctor because they were from the same state. In reality it's not the only factor upon which the relationship is based and sustained, but it's the one that made the connection. Prior to my interviewing this doctor's patients they weren't using that little fact in their marketing, but after hearing it from quite a few patients you can bet they stuck it in their subsequent marketing pieces. Dan Kennedy calls this dog whistle language. That which is only heard by the people it's most important to. It's important to understand with this particular practice, they're located in the New England area of the United States. So, the likelihood of other patients being from the same state are very high. Had this doctor's practice been in California it wouldn't be as powerful a marketing point, unless he was specializing and interested in attracting only former New Englanders; which could be a niche market if pursued.

Another dental client of mine is a retired US Army Lieutenant Colonel having served during Operation Iraqi Freedom. It took me nearly 6 years to convince her this honored period of her past would serve her well in attracting patients.

Another client, not in the dental field uses his former military career as a point of affinity with potential clients. Don Meusser owns a company outside Cleveland, Ohio that sells automatic sliding, folding and revolving doors to commercial construction. Don is a Vietnam Veteran and today we use this fact to attract prospective clients who value this status. Originally, we stumbled upon this by accident. While producing a documentary video about his company and interviewing a number of clients, during the project Don sent me a fax. Atop the fax, in small print, was the line, "A Vietnam Veteran Owned Company". It was the only place I'd ever seen this statement. It wasn't on any other literature, just typed atop the fax cover sheet. Today we use it in subtle ways. Recently I talked with Don about his use of this "affinity" trigger, and he tells me he's connecting with more influential people, also with military backgrounds or ties to the military. Because of his history as a veteran, it has ultimately led to securing large 6-figure projects.

With one particular project Don was bidding against 2 competitors. The CEO of the prospective client received Don's quote, saw he was a Vietnam Veteran and picked up the phone and personally called him and asked of his military service. It turned out this CEO also served in Vietnam about the same time as Don in a nearby unit. On that call the CEO informed Don he'd get the project. Don asked about the other bidders, to which the CEO's response was, *"We both served in Vietnam, I can trust you"*. Your personal connection with prospective patients can be very powerful, but only if you're using it.

There's no telling what piece of your personality, interests, or past will attract others so you should use as much of it as you can. I have a very specific system I've created when working with private clients to help draw out these trust triggers. I remember something a sales trainer once said that stuck with me: "*Every client has a hot button; the one thing that is most important to them and when they find the vendor who pushes that hot button, they'll have their attention and everyone else who leaves it out of their presentation will never stand a chance in closing the sale.*"

People make decisions for their own reasons. In many industries, dentistry included, you're becoming a victim of commoditization and price battles with competitors. When price is the only comparison of value upon which a patient has to judge then price will be their only tool. It's your job to give them other benefits to measure value. Your *'reason why'* is a value that will serve you well only if you use it in your marketing. On this asset alone you will attract patients; you'll also repel some, though they wouldn't be patients you'd want and would ultimately waste time and resources on.

CHAPTER 3

WHY VIDEO TESTIMONIALS?

Before I answer this question, there's more you need to understand about video before I can answer it. You should understand what makes video work before you can be successful using it.

I've been around video and video marketing for more than 29 years and in that time I've witnessed an interesting, yet unchanging dichotomy when it comes to video. When I worked with the fortune 500 companies, Goodyear, Eveready and Harley Davidson for example, they knew video was a medium they should be using to communicate to their audiences, but didn't understand why. On the other side of the fence were the small and mid-sized businesses, which too knew they should be using video, but again, didn't understand why.

Then and now, I start every project by asking the client, *"What's your objective for creating this video? When all is said and done, what do you want your target audience to know, understand, and do from experiencing your video message?"* Often times, I get a blank stare. For almost 3 decades I've been helping businesses create video programs and they consistently do so based on the premise of, *"We know video is powerful, we know we should be using it, we know our target market responds to it, but we don't fully know why."* The majority of people create videos because they see other businesses doing it, having success with it so that's a good enough reason to use it themselves.

The real questions you should ask yourself before implementing video into your marketing are:

- Should we use video?
- Who's our target audience for it?
- Do they want it?
- Will they respond to it?
- What do we want to accomplish with it?

Communication is a 3-Legged Stool

Video marketing posses a lot of virtues, but unless you know what those virtues are, taking the "broad brush" approach to your marketing and applying it will only frustrate you and probably cost you a lot of money. I've lost count of how many people I've met over the years who told me *"Our business is different. We tried video and it didn't work."* These are the same people who blindly jumped in with both feet and created a video because that's what their competitor did and it worked for them... so, if it worked for them, it should work for us. WRONG!!!

With that said, I'll tell you what video is...

Video is a communication medium. It's the second most powerful communication medium, second only to an old fashion face to face, belly to belly, toe to toe conversation or presentation. The one thing video lacks from an in-person conversation is interaction. You don't have the ability to get a viewer to respond to you. You can ask a question and they can respond, but you not being with them to interpret, question, redirect or respond doesn't do you any good.

To fully understand why video is an effective communication medium, you must understand effective communication. For my purpose, effective communication is getting your desired end result. In the case of marketing, advertising and selling, it's making the sale.

Just so we're clear, here's Webster's definition of communication.

Com-mu-ni-cate \ **1**\ An act or instance of transmitting \ **2a:** information communicated b: a verbal or written message \ **3a:** A process by which information is exchanged between individuals through a common system of symbols, signs or information \ **b:** personal rapport.

Here are the key take-aways from the definition:

1. Transmitting (thoughts, ideas, experiences, emotions, stories)
2. Verbal (through sound as well as sight)

3. Exchange between individuals through common... (connection)
4. Personal rapport

Hold that thought! Let's look at the components of effective communication; effective meaning accomplishing your ultimate result.

Effective Communication (Leg 1 of the stool)

A UCLA professor conducted an experiment looking at the 3 components of communication and their impact of effectively transmitting or transferring a thought or idea between individuals. Here's what was learned:

- 55% of effective communication is in the non-verbal exchange
- 38% of effective communication is in the verbal exchange
- 7% of effective communication is in the words you say

More than half of what you "say" is communicated to others through your facial expression, physical demeanor and body language. More than 1/3 based on your voice tone, pace and inflection. And a very small margin in the actual words you say.

I grew up around big dogs, German Sheppard's, Huskies and Boxers, though this is true for any animal. If you said to your pet, *"You're my best friend in the whole world"* with a smile on your face and an upbeat, excited tone in your voice then your pet will respond with excitement. But, if you said the same phrase with your face scrunched up with a mean looking scowl and a harsh scolding tone in your voice, they're likely to cower from you. The words are the same, but the non-verbal aspect and voice tone has changed; therefore the "communication" (the transfer of information) is completely different.

Understanding this is more critical today than ever before. Your audience's attention is less focused. People have their noses buried in their smart phones, talking on the telephone, pressed up to computer screens checking their email and to see what friends are saying on Facebook. What you communicate with your body language and voice is far more important than what you actually say. You have to expect that people are only half paying attention to your message, along with the 3699+ other messages they're being bombarded with each day.

That's the quick and dirty of understanding how to communicate with your audience, but it's only one part of the equation. I said people are only half listening to you, next you need to know the psychological behaviors of your buyer.

Buying Behavior (Leg 2 of the stool)

In the previous section I discussed how information is effectively communicated, leg 1 of the stool. In most selling situations a purchase is rarely made on first contact. Most people have certain behaviors, or buying cycles, they go through before they decide to buy. Most often, the larger the investment the longer the cycle.

It's important to understand the stages of the patient's buying cycle, and that certain senses have dominance over others in retaining information. This isn't intended to be an extensive lesson on how people buy, but understanding why video is effective in influencing and persuading people.

For example purposes, here are the 5 behaviors people go through in reaching a buying decision.

1. Problem recognition:
    a. We recognize we have a problem and seek a solution. I.E. You're hungry, seek out food.
2. Information gathering:
    a. What options are available that can solve your problem?
3. Evaluation:
    a. Processing information gathered about the solution options
4. Purchase decision:
    a. Narrowing and selecting solution options (product, service, vendor, payment options, etc.)

      b. Product/service, credibility, experience, availability, warranties, guarantees, social proof, trust, etc impacts final decision

5. Post Purchase evaluation:

      a. Are you satisfied or dissatisfied with the product or service? Product/service abandonment is recognized as "buyer's remorse" in selling.

Retention (Leg 3 of the stool)

All communication is received, processed and retained through the 5 senses; sight, sound, smell, taste and touch. It's important to understand which of the senses is more dominate with regard to how your patients retain what you communicate to them and how they process it through their buying behavior.

Studies show that sight and sound are the senses through which you retain the majority of what is communicated to you. Here's how information retention is divided amongst your 5 senses.

You retain…

- 83% of what you SEE
- 11% of what you HEAR
- 3% of what you SMELL
- 2% of what you TOUCH
- 1% of what you TASTE

Overlay the retention statistics with the effective communication stats and you'll have a clear picture why video is an effective communication tool in persuading your audience.

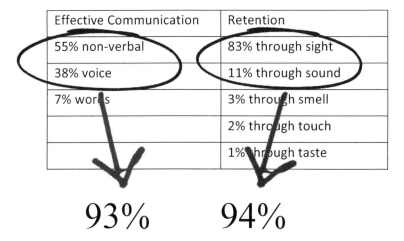

Effective Communication	Retention
55% non-verbal	83% through sight
38% voice	11% through sound
7% words	3% through smell
	2% through touch
	1% through taste

93%   94%

93% of effective communication is in the sight and sound and you retain 94% of what you see and hear.

I know all this was probably painful; stats, behaviors, blah, blah, blah. All you wanted to know is why video is a powerfully persuasive marketing tool and how you can leverage it. I'm getting to that.

What They <u>DON'T</u> Tell You About Video

Now for the cold hard truth about video; because you can't interact with your audience in video it cannot close a sale for you. It CAN introduce you to them, win them over with your stunning personality, demonstrate all your benefits and value, it can bring them to the brink of saying yes to your treatments, but it cannot make them accept them.

In nearly 3 decades of producing persuasive videos I've never had a sale closed by the video. Don't get me wrong, it can get them close, but you're still going to have to seal the deal.

A friend and client of mine owns a bricks and mortar retail vacuum store and is very effective at using video to sell vacuums. In fact his average sale is around $800, and he's had people drive as far away as 100 miles to buy from him. In the videos, he gives a complete demonstration of individual vacuum models, which allows the buyers to see each without the pressure of being "sold."

The secret sauce for him to get people to drive past dozens of other vacuum stores is his personality; on video, he's a real person buyers come to know, like, and trust. Don't get me wrong, he's a very good salesperson. He used to sell vacuums door to door, face to face, which is what makes him lethal on video. His strategy, technique, and persona are multiplied via video.

Persuasive Video Marketing is in the Psychology Not the Technology

Video is a bright shiny object. Like computers, the technology is changing constantly. Unfortunately too many people, my video and production peers included, put too much emphasis on the "toys" that make the video rather than the psychology that goes into its creation. That brings me back to the start of this chapter when I said people identified that they needed to do video because others were applying it with success; entirely the wrong reason. It's an incestuous cesspool of the blind leading the blind. You cannot afford to get caught in this circle.

Video allows you to consistently communicate and demonstrate your products, services, marketing messages and ideas to a large audience simultaneously. Your message can be distributed on DVD, the Internet, on TV and Cable TV, and played in the waiting room of your practice. It allows you to multiply your marketing efforts, rather than divide your time.

It puts you in front of your existing patients and prospective patients, almost as if you were there in person. So that it's not overlooked, personal rapport is the one key component from Webster's definition of communication that I have not yet discussed... for strategic reason. Personal rapport is the one component you must include in all your marketing. People don't buy from businesses, they buy from people they know like and trust. Former Heavy Weight Boxing Champion and successful entrepreneur George Foreman states, *"People don't buy what's in your hand, they buy you. Once people buy you they'll buy what you sell."*

How do people buy you? You can tell them about you, but that's called bragging and can turn people off; but if others talk about you its social proof. What others say about you is 1000 times more powerful than what you can say about you. And, unfortunately, your prospects will believe what a complete stranger has to say about you more than they will you.

Finally, that brings me to video testimonials.

Video testimonials encapsulate all the psychological components of video I've discussed so far, plus the added weapon of social proof. It's the opportunity for your prospect to see, hear, and experience what others say about you in a convenient, convincing manner. Remember, effective communication and retention takes the best form in sight and sound.

Even more powerful is your prospect's ability to connect with what patients say. It's premature at this point to go into detail, other than to say prospects will connect with what your patients say about you and their experience with you. We influence through connection.

Through video testimonials, preferably multiple testimonials, you create the opportunity for prospects to connect or relate to other people and their problems. To connect with others it's important they view you to be like them, though you must be authentic. Unfortunately if not done right, you can be perceived as phony. However testimonials are perceived legitimately, and when captured properly, create tremendous credibility for you.

Your objective with every patient should be to create a mutually beneficial relationship; a relationship both of you benefit from. A successful relationship is based on a successive series of positive outcomes.

Think about the dating process. For the person looking for a serious personal relationship, they need to build the relationship on trust, over time, instead of asking them to jump in bed on the first date. Applying aggressive selling tactics can get you quick sales, but it won't bring you lasting, profitable patients. Selling is about seduction, and video testimonials are a marketing tool that you can effectively apply to seduce prospective patients and reinforce existing patients of the value in maintaining their relationship with you.

What video testimonials do for your practice?

- **Builds a bond of trust:** It's a fact of life that we do business with those we trust. But these days, tooting your own horn too much can submarine your marketing effort. Conversely, when a prospect watches a video testimonial about your practice from a complete stranger, it's considered objective feedback…an d so, it's more believable.

- **Improves credibility:** Having credible testimonials from patients who are advocates connects those patients to prospective ones. I call this connection a transfer of trust between patients, but also creating trust in you.

- **Demonstrates success:** When you develop a head-turning video testimonial, your prospect *feels* the success you've created for others. First-time patients will want you as their dentist because they want the outcome you created for others like them.

- **Trust by proxy:** Because you're a doctor, many patients cannot identify or relate with you. In their minds you're at a higher position, similar to celebrities, because you have a skill and knowledge level they themselves don't posses, therefore it makes it challenging to see you as an average person, you're superior. When you follow my model for testimonials, other patients share their stories of their own personal experiences, and how you were able to help them. In turn, the prospective patient understands that they are in the same situation as your other patients; having the same fears, anxieties, or dental concerns. Therefore, because you were able to help your others like them and you can help them too.

The bulk of this book will focus on how to capture and leverage every ounce of marketing power out of your video testimonials.

Chapter 4

PATIENT TESTIMONIALS IN YOUR PRACTICE

Selling is something neither dentists nor patients like taking part in. Unfortunately it is a necessary evil to get the patient from no case, to case acceptance. There is however a strategy that can prepare a patient, in advance, for a case presentation.

In addition to the potentially large investment a patient can expect on a case, there are a lot of other small details that go into the patient's decision making. The 2 largest are fear and trust. I've interviewed hundreds of dental patients and between 85 & 90 percent of all patients have had a poor or bad experience with a dentist in their past. They're afraid of duplicating that experience. For many patients they'd rather avoid seeing a dentist all together; and many go years or decades between visits. It's inevitable that we all must see a dentist at some point or another, either to fix a problem or prevent one. Prevention is cheaper, but that's not a very good marketing message.

So how can you convince prospective patients that you're not "scary", and they won't re-live past experiences in your office? Let them see and hear what it's like to be a patient in your practice before they make the commitment to become one. In an earlier chapter, I provided you with a specific strategy on how to do this, but here I want to address the tactical aspect of it. The most effective way is to use patient testimonials; more specifically, video testimonials.

You're probably thinking one of two things at this point; you have patient testimonials or, you've tried to get them and haven't been successful at it. In this chapter you'll discover how I do it and you can adapt my method to your practice. Before I get into the tactics, it's important to identify where you are on my testimonial model.

Where Are You?

I've been at this game of video marketing, or more specifically, capturing video testimonials for more than 30 years. I've identified 3 distinct groups of people/businesses when it comes to testimonials. As you read these, decide which category you are because it'll tell us where you need to start in your patient testimonial strategy.

A true testimony is a statement of endorsement about you and your practice. For the practice, the most effective testimonies will speak to the dentist's ability to solve the patient's problem, caring, and ability to create cases that satisfy the patient's need and/or want. Patients however, when asked without directions and guidance, will often speak entirely of their personal feelings about the dentist and team they see during treatment. This is ok, but it's a small aspect of a highly effective testimony, and will severally limit your ability to leverage the testimonies in preparing your prospective patients for accepting your case presentations.

The first group is unaware of testimonials. A private client of mine, Donna Krech, is in the health and wellness business. She runs several multi-million dollar companies, and each of them are driven entirely on testimonial-based marketing and advertising. Donna shared a story about a speaking engagement to a group of businesswoman, where one of her private coaching clients described an event she was holding for the public. All of a sudden, from across the room, another lady shouted how fabulous these events were and if people didn't take advantage of the opportunity, they were really missing out. Unfortunately Donna's coaching client didn't recognize this unsolicited testimony for what it was, and secondly didn't capitalize on seeking out her public advocate to capture her testimony in a recorded form. Do you recognize testimonials when someone says something about you? Do you have a plan or system for capturing and leveraging them? If not, you're in this first category…and that's okay.

There's a saying: *"You don't know what you don't know"* or to put it a different way, *"you're only aware of things you're aware of; you're not aware of things you're not aware of"*. After reading this, I guarantee you'll become more aware of them.

The second group notices and is aware of testimonials, but doesn't see the parallels with their own practice. If they do make the connection, they don't know how to go about using testimonials in all aspects of their marketing. They acknowledge their existence, but they don't know what to do with them.

Finally, the third group is actually using testimonies, but not as effectively or extensively as they could. In fact, I'm not sure there's anyone who's really leveraging testimonials to the degree that they should. I mentioned Donna Krech, she's brilliant at using testimonials, but even she knows she's not getting all the mileage out of them that she could.

So which group are you in? Do you miss testimonials when they happen? Do you recognize them, but haven't figured out how to incorporate them into your practice? Or are you using them and want to know how to leverage them more for greater marketing effectiveness

The Little Hinge

Little hinges swing big doors; small changes can make big differences. I'm a student of psychology and language. I hold 2 certifications in hypnotherapy and have been a practicing hypnotist for more than 32 years. I was fortunate to have had a personal mentor in hypnosis, and I remember early in my training he told me that to be good at hypnosis, I had to have a command of the English language.

When we say or hear the word 'testimony' it conjures up an idea in people. Think about it. When you ask a patient for a testimonial, what thought process does it create in them? Put yourself in their shoes. If I said to you, *"Would you mind giving us a testimonial?"* As a dentist, you're a respected figure in your community and I'm sure you've been asked this before. What was your instinctive, emotional reaction the moment the question was asked? And what if you were asked to give a testimonial to a faceless, emotionless, non-responsive video camera? Now the nerves start to race and you can feel the sweat begin to pour.

I've worked with a lot of dentists and I know you have an analytical mind. If you can get past the fear of being on camera, your mind starts to think about what you're going to say. You're suddenly put on the spot. You may not know what to say so the fight or flight instinct kicks in. Your patients feel the same thing. You're asking the patient to *"perform"*. Most people's perception of a testimonial is to say great things about you, so that's exactly what they do, but that's not what I think a great testimonial is.

I believe there are 2 types of testimonials; the *survey* and the *documentary*. The survey testimonial is what most dental practices get from their patients. Here are actual patient testimonials from dental websites that I picked randomly. I lifted the testimonials without identifying the practice, site or patients in order to protect their identity. Notice the consistency in the content of the testimonies.

"Dr. XXXX is the best dentist I've ever been to. He treats you like you are a friend and delivers excellent quality of work. I will not go anywhere else to get my teeth worked on again. "

"Everything was very professional, there was no waiting time in the lobby and I was taken right away for my cleaning."

"Oddly enough, I have always looked forward to seeing all of you. How many people can say that about going to the dentist's office?"

"To be able to trust someone with your friends and/or family is very important to me. I trust each and every person working in your office... having known you and your son for years now, I have complete confidence in everything you do."

"I think you are amazing."

There's nothing wrong with these testimonials, but what's missing from them? I consider these <u>survey</u> testimonials. They're what you'd get if you surveyed your patients. They're the product of poor or no questioning. If you just let the patient talk, they'll say what they think you want them to say. I call this *"verbal vomit"*; saying whatever comes to mind. Getting these types of testimonials will severely limit how and where you can use them, and do very little to boost your marketing. They're of little marketing nutritional value for you. For your prospective patients and me, these testimonials are superficial. They're missing the real story behind what brought the patient to say this. They are <u>incomplete testimonials</u>.

The second type of testimonial is a documentary. A documentary in the film sense is a 'telling' of reality. It's nonfiction. It's a story. In today's economy your patients are cynical toward formal marketing. When you can capture your patient's story, you harness the power of their experiences and leverage the power of *affinity*. Affinity is what 2 or more people share in common. In the case of using patient testimonials, it's what your patient and a prospective patient may share, specifically their past experiences with dentistry or their dental situations. For example, a prospective patient who's had a horrible dental experience in the past, and hears an existing patient who's shared the same experience, can connect with them on that point, or simply put; 2 patients who share the same fears and anxieties. When your patient shares their story and a prospective patient connects with that story, you win by proxy. When your existing patient had these troubles and you fixed it, or made it possible to solve their situation, and the prospective patient has a similar situation, the dots are connected. The prospective patients sees it as; "you helped that patient who had my problem therefore, you can help me". It's powerful marketing and the best part is, it doesn't appear as marketing at all.

To be truly effective, your target audience must believe the testimonial to be authentic. When they believe it to be authentic, it elevates your credibility and that of all your marketing. There's one specific strategy I've started implementing with my private dental clients that's significantly increased their credibility and authority.

Let me close the loop on the difference between survey and documentary type testimonials. The significant difference between each is in questioning. If you want different answers, you have to ask different questions.

Language is Important

Earlier I said I'm a student of language. Your success in getting testimonials and video testimonials is entirely dependent on the language you use. Here's what's happening in your practice right now, whether you're getting testimonials or not; anxiety and apprehension is taking place. Either your patients, or your staff, or both, are feeling anxiety and apprehension about testimonials and it's all created because of the wrong language. The word testimonial is the problem. Eliminate it from your language. Instead of asking patients to give you *testimonials* about their experience with you, ask them to *share* their thoughts, comments, feelings, or experiences of being a patient in your practice. Exchange the word **testimonial** with the word **share**. The word *share* doesn't create the uneasiness in your team or patient that the word *testimonial* does.

The old adage is, "How do you get a testimonial? Ask. We want it to be easy. However, there's more psychology behind getting a great testimonial than simply asking for one. First, change how you ask then employ a strategy behind getting a documentation style testimonial.

I've had many dentists and their dental hygienists tell me of their anxiety asking patients for testimonials, but none as articulate as Donna. Donna is a dental hygienist with a private client in upstate New York. Dr. Pearce is a very smart marketer. He understands the power of relationship marketing and decided to make patient video testimonials an important part of his marketing. They hold weekly marketing meetings to discuss strategies to promote and advance the business. While at his office filming their documentary film about the practice, Donna explained how they were incentivized to record patient video testimonials, but despite the financial compensation, she had trouble getting past the "*icky*" feeling (her words) of asking a patient for a video testimonial. Questioning her further, she felt it was outside the comfort zone of the relationship she and the patients shared. I asked when and how she asked patients. She asked at the right time when a patient expressed gratitude or positive feedback, but it was *how* she asked that created the problem. When a patient would say something worthy of asking for a testimonial, she asked, *"Would you give us a video testimonial?"*

In the next chapter I'll share the system I've developed, that I shared with Donna and made the difference for her. I get paid a great deal of money by private clients to recruit patients and record their extensive testimonial stories and I share my system.

Chapter 5

MY SYSTEM FOR CAPTURING PERSUASIVE PATIENT TESTIMONIALS

It starts with recognizing when to ask. Donna had been trained how to recognize when to ask. The best time is when the patient is in the 'glow'. The glow is often immediately after they've experienced the benefits of being a patient. It may be their first treatment visit with you. They may have come to the office with anxiety and you put them at ease right away. Or, you may have completed their smile reconstruction and they're seeing their 'new' self for the very first time. You know it. It's the exuberant smile they've never shown before. They can't hold it back, it just happens. There may be tears of joy. They may say something like: *"You guys are miracle workers." "I didn't think it was possible to have the smile I've always dreamed of." "I never liked coming to the dentist, but you're different."* I consider these testimonial triggers. You'll recognize these statements similar to the examples I showed earlier. Most would stop here and think they have a good testimonial, but I want to dig deeper for the whole story. That will serve you better as a marketing tool.

[For the language and script I teach clients how to ask for a testimonial is be found on the resource website companion with this book at www.BookOnTestimonials.com]

If you're interested only in written testimonials then my scripting will serve you well. If you want to leverage patient testimonials for all that you can, then you'll want them on video. Introducing video and/or audio recording adds another level to the system. Here is what I shared with Donna to help her get past the "icky" feeling of asking a patient for a video testimonial. The tweak was changing one word in how she asked.

[You'll find the entire 'tweak' I taught Donna on the resource website at www.BookOnTestimonials.com]

Who Should Capture The Testimonials?

I'm often asked who should actually record the testimonial; the doctor or a team member? I believe the doctor can ask the patient to share their thoughts and comments, but it's not his or her place to actually capture them. The odds of the patient agreeing to share their experiences will increase significantly when the doctor facilitates it, but the doc should not actually perform the task of recording it. This is best left to your team. The dental team often has a greater personal rapport and interaction with the patients.

Incorporating testimonials into your marketing shouldn't be taken lightly. Aside from the marketing benefits testimonials can provide, they're also part of your patient's experience with you and your practice. If you're providing an excellent patient experience then patients will be telling their friends and family about your practice, even referring them to you. This is *"word of mouth marketing"*, as is testimonial marketing. My point is that patient testimonials are similar to referrals, in that your patients are advocates for you in telling other people about your virtues. Testimonials facilitate that message from one to many that you control. Again, how you do that is all part of their experience with you.

Additionally, an amazing thing happens when a patient articulates their thoughts and experiences with you. They know what it's like to be your patient, but when they verbalize it and hear themselves saying it, it solidifies their belief in their experience. It's one thing to think it; it's another to voice it. A powerful transformation takes place when your patients state out loud how much they love you and your practice. Once you help them articulate it, you're also training them on how to tell others about you. Few people give deep thought to their feelings of something or someone. For most it remains a feeling; helping them articulate their feelings helps affirm their decisions.

To Get Different Responses, Ask Different Questions

By now you understand the difference between a survey and a documentary style testimonial. The difference is in the questions you ask. So what questions do you ask? That will depend on 2 things; the objections you're presently getting, and the objectives you want to achieve.

If you're doing tooth by tooth dentistry and want to perform more of the kind of dentistry you love doing but are struggling to get patients to commit to your treatment plans, then your questions must lead to answering the objections you're getting. If you're already doing cases but want to increase the size and profit of the cases, again, what obstacles are you facing?

First start with the objections you're hearing from prospective patients who aren't buying from you. What is preventing them from saying yes to your case presentations?

Second, what benefits do patients experience by being a patient in your practice? You don't want to script your patient's testimonials because they'll be your words, not theirs and therefore, not authentic. You do however want to define for yourself what you want them to say, and structure your questioning toward getting them to say that. I said it earlier and it's worth saying again; many people don't know how to articulate themselves, you have to help them and it's your questioning that will do that. To ask a patient to give you a testimonial is asking them to do all the work. Instead, create a conversation with your patient and capture it on video and/or audio. You should implement a testimonial program, but you should NOT be the one to capture them. You can however, facilitate the entire process by encouraging patients to give them. I tell patients I interview there are no right or wrong answers; I want to hear about their experiences, good or bad. You ask the questions and all you want in return are their answers; spontaneous, honest answers.

The questions must always be open ended forcing the patient to articulate. Never ask a question the patient can answer with a simple "yes" or "no". For example, *"Has your experience as a patient with our practice been a good one?"* Instead ask, *"Tell me about your experiences as a patient with us."* This will enable patients to explain their experiences in their own language and words, not yours. You are not your patients; you'd explain things differently than they will. That's because your position in the experience is different. You're the dentist administering the service and they're the patients who experience the benefits of it...good or bad! Their perspective is a thousand times more relevant than yours. That's why patient testimonials are so powerful. Your patients will speak in your prospective patient's language. Capturing and sharing powerful patient testimonials is putting your advocate patients to work for you without putting them on the marketing payroll.

The 300 pound Video Testimonial Gorilla

Why won't people give you a video testimonial? To be completely fair this question has to be answered from two sides; yours and your patients.

There's no doubt people have an aversion to giving a video testimonial, but often for different reasons. I've found the biggest challenge in getting a video testimonial has more to do with what's going on in your or your patient's head than any physical obstacle. If you think you can or can't get a video testimonial from your patients, in either case, you're right.

You first have to believe it's possible to get video testimonials from patients. I have a countless number of clients on both sides of the fence; those who know they can and get them repeatedly, and those who think they can't, and never do. Your success (or failure) in capturing them has a lot to do with what you project to the patient in non-verbal communication when you ask.

If you ask with hesitancy then the patient's going to be hesitant to give it; but if you ask with confidence, the patient is more likely to be persuaded to comply. Understand, I didn't say if asked with confidence they'll comply without hesitation. But its far easier to persuade them if you believe it possible.

During the development of a marketing video I did for a client, I made the observation that all of their marketing was void of client testimonials… to which the owner said, *"We've tried to get them!"* My response was, *"either the wrong person is asking, or you're asking the wrong way."* Point being, because he didn't believe it possible to "get" testimonials, based on past experience, then every person he asked, he expected a negative response from. For me, the surprising thing was, this came from a very successful entrepreneur and highly skilled direct sales person.

There's a lesson here. When asking for testimonials, especially video testimonials, you have to fight your own mindset about the subject.

Let's consider your mindset first. These are typical responses I get from my clients when I ask them about capturing testimonials:

- I don't like being on camera, so my patients won't like it

- I've asked before and kept getting "no" for an answer

- I'm afraid to ask

Five Reasons Patients Say "No"

There are several inhibitors that stop a person from giving you a video testimonial.

- **A patients' own mindset:** When you ask a patient to give you a video testimonial, the self confidence barrier automatically comes up and they feel unqualified to participate. You must reinforce the fact that they are the perfect person to talk to other patients with similar concerns, just like theirs.
- **YOUR mindset:** Your own mindset, and how you ask for a video testimonial has a lot to do with how your patient reacts. Put yourself in their place; the fact that you wouldn't go in front of the camera, you think they wouldn't want to do so either. Therefore, you are projecting the outcome. What you hold in your mind determines your results…change your mindset about video testimonials and getting in front of the camera, and you will achieve the results you want.
- **Being "camera shy":** When you ask patients to do a video testimonial, all they can think about is getting in front of the camera, which most people don't like to do and will avoid at any cost. Often times, people get hung up on how they look,

or how they sound, and will politely decline; no matter how happy they are being your patient.

- **Content:** Asking a patient for a testimonial is similar to asking them for a referral. If you ask the client for a referral in a broad sense, they have their whole world to choose from, and have difficulty thinking of a single person to refer. But, if you ask them in a more targeted way, such as; "*do you know someone in your Rotary Club who would be in need of my services?*", you now have pared down their list of possible candidates to think of, making it much easier for them to help you. It's the same thing with asking them to give a testimonial. If you simply ask them "*can you give us a testimonial?*"; they are left to try and figure out what to say…right then and there (a very uncomfortable situation to be in)…and will usually come up with things like "*Oh, they're great; they're really nice people and I like going there*". However, if you ask the right questions, and help lead the conversation, you'll get more powerful testimonials you can really use, and will make a difference in your marketing.

- **Commitment:** When you ask a patient for video testimonials you are asking them to make a commitment. Adding their name to your patient and vouching for your service, dedication and results. Even though everything they will say about you is true, they are still cautious about endorsing a product or service.

Ron Sheetz

Chapter 6

THE LOST ART OF PERSONAL CONNECTION

In my grandparent's day it wasn't uncommon to hear a knock on the door of their home in the middle of the day. Often times it was a neighbor borrowing a cup of sugar to bake cookies (which they always brought in exchange for the borrowed sugar).

In my mom's day, the knocks on the door were less frequent, but still happened, especially on the nights she taught dance classes out of our home basement. It also wasn't uncommon for the neighbor kid to come knocking to ask me to come out and play.

Today, it's different. A knock on the door at my house usually means a solicitor is calling. We've never had the neighbor kids ask our kids out to play, and never has a neighbor knocked on our door asking to borrow a cup of sugar. In fact, we know very little about our neighbors.

The point is the "sociability" of people has changed significantly through the generations. In my grandparent's era, social media was getting together at the dining room table over a cup of coffee and cookies; today it's smart phones, texting, Facebook, Twitter, LinkedIn, Pinterest and YouTube. Has technology made us more or less sociable? I think less; my neighbors barely say hi across our fenced in yards, but they probably wouldn't bat an eye at sending me a text hello. That wouldn't require any interpersonal interaction.

On December 30, 2012, the front page of USA Today posted an article titled "The Year We Stopped Talking." "93% of the population now uses cell phones or wireless devices..." "The downside: Often, we're effectively disconnecting from those in the same room."

Let's shift the focus to business. I learned sales techniques and strategies very early on; the Ben Franklin close, the assumptive close, asking alternate choice questions rather than close-ended questions. In fact, I produced an entire series of video sales training programs for Lighthouse Pools (a recreation retailer in the Cleveland, Ohio area selling above-ground pools, hot tubs and billiard tables) in which we taught scripted presentations (specific to each product in the store) that started the moment the customer entered the store. Every step of the interaction was choreographed to manipulate and influence the customer. There's nothing better than face to face selling; unfortunately it's not possible with every patient, unless you employ video testimonials. It's the next best thing to presenting face to face. Additionally, for the potential patients, it's safe because it can't 'pressure' them and 'take' money from them; or so they may think. It is then, the next best marketing tool at your disposal to establish relationship and build rapport with your target patients.

Chapter 7

TESTIMONIALS ARE THE ORIGINAL SOCIAL MEDIA

The buzz about Facebook, YouTube, Twitter and others being ***THE*** social media is a lie. There's nothing *social* about them. Merriam Webster defines "social" as:

so·cial *adjective* \ˈsō-shəl\

: relating to or involving activities in which people spend time talking to each other or doing enjoyable things with each other

: liking to be with and talk to people : happy to be with people

: of or relating to people or society in general

Quite honestly, they're "bright shiny marketing objects" right now; and there's a lot of competition for that space. The closest these media get to being social is *"relating to people or society in general."* This is where I'll start.

Patient testimonials have been considered social media (likely the original social media); more accurately, they're true social *proof.* To be more specific in regards to our discussion here, I'm referring to *video testimonials*.

Once again, deferring to Merriam Webster for a definition:

proof *noun* \ˈprüf\

: something which shows that something else is true or correct

Combine the 2 definitions and you have:

relating to people or society in general, something which shows that something else is true or correct...

... and you have testimonials, or, *true social proof.*

Patient testimonials are easy to get and you can re-purpose them anywhere and everywhere in your practice advertising and marketing.

Throughout this book, I refer to video testimonials because video is the medium in which I do most of my work. However, it's important to understand that you can adapt all the information contained in this book to testimonials in any form, visual, spoken or written.

The traditional model for capturing a video testimonial is to ask your patient for one, they say yes and you stick a Flip camera in front of them. This is asking them to get psychologically and emotionally naked in front of a camera. Most people's "knee jerk" reaction is to say no; it's like walking into a retail store and the clerk asks, *"Can I help you?"* Your instinctive response is, *"No, I'm just looking."* Those patients that agree to give you a testimonial may have the best intentions, but unfortunately, they're going to babble off the first thing that comes to mind. Even though they'll say wonderful things about you and your practice, these types of testimonials limit your ability to use them in your marketing.

Don't leave crafting the message of the testimonial to your patients... they're not qualified to tell your story, your way. You can get them to say exactly what you want if you know the formula behind it. First, draft a list of objections and questions you're often asked about your services during a sales presentation. What pains do you solve for patients? I'll start with "Testimonial Triggers." Testimonial triggers are to a marketer, what "buying signs" are to a direct sales person. They identify the very moment the patient will be the most agreeable to giving you a powerfully persuasive testimonial.

Ron Sheetz

Chapter 8

TESTIMONIAL TRIGGERS

I've already stated how to get testimonials…you ask. My contention is; even though there are right and wrong times to ask a patient for a testimonial, the key is in <u>how</u> you ask for one. I'll address the how later, but for now, when should you ask? The best time to ask is when the patient is in what I call the "*glow*"; they're feeling good about you, their experience, or the results of what you've done. There are opportunities when the "right time" presents itself, to ask your patient for a video testimonial. I call these times *testimonial triggers*. In other words, recognizing the signs should "trigger" your response in asking for the testimonial.

I remember having dinner at a restaurant called Stir Crazy (an Asian restaurant) with my sister and brother-in-law who were visiting from Orlando. It's a place we enjoy going to when they're in town. Past visits to the restaurant are a blur, other than the company we shared. The food's good, but I couldn't tell you what I ordered in past visits, let alone our waiter or waitresses' names. On this particular night, our waiter was Ryan; he was fantastic, and his service and manner were impeccable. Not only was he attentive to our every need; he also casually and strategically learned the names of all 11 people in my party, including my kids, and then used them throughout the evening. Not once but continuously. By the end of the meal, it felt as if he knew us, and we him. It was as if he'd been our regular waiter for years, like the staff on the TV series *Cheers*; greeting the regular customers by their first name. His attention and service improved our experience in the restaurant and the food immensely.

The end result was that I gladly left a significantly higher tip because he improved our experience... it was Disney-like; even referring to my daughter as princess. We were so pleased with him we asked to see the manager, who approached our table sheepishly, not knowing what to expect. Pay attention, here's the testimonial trigger: We expressed how fantastic the meal was because of Ryan and his service. It was a casual comment. My wife and mother raved about him, sharing specific details about him. The manager's response, *"Thank you, it's always nice to hear positive comments!"* He missed the opportunity for us to give a formal testimonial, let alone a video one, which we'd have gladly done had he been prepared to do so. If we were to return 3 days later and the manager recognized us and then asked for a formal testimonial he'd have gotten it, but not as expressively articulate as immediately after the experience. The emotional engagement wouldn't be the same and the verbalization of the experience wouldn't be as heart-felt. The opportunity was missed. You don't want to miss these opportunities with your patients.

Testimonial Triggers are more about a moment expressed by your patients, than anything they say specifically; though their words can clearly indicate they're primed for asking to share their thoughts and experiences.

It's a lot like love. How do you know you're in love? You just know it, and you'll know it when your patients are in the right frame of mind to share their feelings with you or your team.

Testimonial triggers can happen at the desk when the patient is done with their appointment, or it could be during casual conversation. It doesn't matter when it happens, you need to be ready to ask, and be prepared to capture it right then and there. I hear all too often from practices that they don't have time; they're too busy. That's fine, but if you stop working on the business to attract more patients then sooner or later, you'll have more time on your hands than you'll know what to do with. Unfortunately, when you have all this time to ask patients, there won't be any to ask. No one ever said running a practice would be easy; easy is a false god.

For the purpose of example, I'll share a few testimonial triggers you're hearing everyday. By no means are these examples all inclusive, there are endless ways a patient can express their readiness to be approached about a testimonial. The most obvious is when a patient compliments you, compares you against other dentists, speaks of telling others about you (referring), complains about another practice, or you overhear them in conversation with another talking about you.

The lesson to be learned is that you should always be on the look out; listening for the chance to get a testimonial from your patients.

Asking For and Getting Video Testimonials

I've already established that you have to be on the look out for testimonial triggers.

Let's say a patient fires one off and it sounds something like this, *"You guys are fantastic! I can't see myself going anywhere else."* Your team must be ready and scripted with a response designed to get the patient to agree upon giving a testimonial.

[See the script I developed in response to testimonial triggers specifically for dental practices at www.BookOnTestimonials.com]

Ron Sheetz

Chapter 9

5 COMPONENTS OF A POWERFUL VIDEO TESTIMONIAL THAT WILL CREATE PHENOMENAL CREDIBILITY

The use of positive client, customer, patient or member testimonials in your marketing and advertising, training is an overlooked and underused tool. For those practices that are using them, they are generally using what I call 'vanilla' testimonials. Most are boring and universally dull and without any nutritional value. Here's a test. If after you read a testimonial can you say, "so what"?

What a satisfied patient can say about you will carry a thousand times more weight with prospective clients than anything you could ever say about yourself. If you promote great things about your practice, it's just bragging. When your patients say it, it's actual experience. There are 5 things that must be included in your testimonials to make them believable and effective as a marketing tool.

The Successful Testimonial Formula

How do you get a testimonial from a patient? Ask! Just ask your best patients if they would tell you, in their own words, why they do chose you and continue to see you. I know what you're thinking. You do have testimonials. Do your testimonials sound something like this?

- "XYZ Dentistry is very reliable and they are great people."

- "Dr. Smith is one of the best dentists you can have. I would recommend him to anyone."

These testimonials are okay and they may serve your ego well, though they won't stand up to the test. They won't stand up to the "so what" and "who cares" test. Prospective customers want to know what's in it for them. How do these testimonials tell your prospective patient how seeing you will make a difference for them?

The most powerful testimonial will include these 5 components. Even if you're able to obtain only one, I guarantee it will be more effective in adding credibility to your marketing than a boring one. The 5 key components:

1. Contain Meaningful Specifics
2. Define Actual Outcomes
3. Answer a patient's objections or satisfy their objectives
4. Reinforce Benefits & Emotions
5. Include Full Names & Details

The best way to obtain your testimonials is on video. You can use them in three different mediums; video, audio, and print…all you need to do is to start asking for them using my scripting. When a patient tells you how great you are be sure you have your tablet or smart phone camera ready to start recording. Just ask them, and they'll give them to you. Customer video testimonials will improve credibility by 1000%.

There is specific methodology behind why and how my scripting works. You will find the complete methodology behind my scripting on the resource site at www.BookOnTestimonials.com

Chapter 10

MAKING A VIDEO TESTIMONIAL POWERFULLY PERSUASIVE

Now that you have a patient who's agreed to go on video and give you a testimonial what do you do next?

You can let them talk extemporaneously or you can guide them with questions. Letting them talk on they're own, making up the content of their testimonial is the easiest for you, but will often produce less than marketable messages. Plus it will usually only give you one message to work with; and it will probably be pretty "vanilla." Just like vanilla ice cream it will be basic and without flavor.

You've worked very hard to get them to agree to appear on video, now's not the time to let them babble on about what a nice person you are. This'll serve your ego, but it doesn't give you much flexibility in your marketing.

Create 5-7 questions you can ask targeted at producing testimonials that can actually help your marketing. Testimonials are social proof; proof that should support your marketing message, overcome patient objections and server your objectives.

What questions should you ask? The answer is specific to your practice, and the treatments and services you provide. What objections or questions do you get from other prospective patients? Have your advocate patients address these objections. Preparing patients with testimonials is more persuasive than if <u>you</u> try to tackle the questions yourself. Look at it from the prospective patient's point of view; in his or her mind, your motives are to sell treatments (extract money from them), and their motives are to not be sold. Therefore, your advocate patients provide testament from a peer that what you say and market is credible.

You ask the question and have your patient respond, spontaneously. There's great power in the spontaneity. Your patient will be perceived by viewers as being real, sincere, conversational and unrehearsed; not as part of a sales pitch, because they're using their own words.

Asking several questions will give you a diverse library of testimonials that you can apply anywhere you need in your marketing. And keep in mind, 1 video testimonial can be applied in multiple mediums. At last count I devised 33 different ways to use 1 video testimonial. Ask 1 client 5 targeted questions and you'll have a resource to be deployed 155 different ways.

Residual Benefits of Video Testimonials (Maximum Marketing Leverage)

You want more patients, but how do you attract more? What do you want? What do your patients want? We all want something, and often the gap in between isn't that wide, yet in the effort to create perfect marketing pieces to attract ideal patients, you can loose sight of what's really important and omit it from your marketing. Getting this right can make the difference in attracting the right patients to you.

If you follow my strategy for cultivating testimonials, you'll end up with an abundance of content and valuable information. As I write this book, I'm completing a very large, long-format, documentary film for a dental client where I interviewed over 30 of their patients. In the 10-30 minute conversations I had with each patient, they revealed everything they loved and didn't like about the dentist and practice. All the positive stuff becomes an endless resource and library of patient testimonials, usable in video, audio, and print form. All the other stuff becomes research for creating future marketing. When asked, your patients will reveal everything you need to know in order to attract more patients just like them; all you have to do is ask. The key is to ask the right questions. Here's an example, and though this may seem an obvious question to ask, it often isn't because it's SO obvious; *"What was it about Dr. Smith that helped you finally decide he/she was the right dentist for you?"* In my present work, I'm hearing some unexpected responses, such as; *"I decided on Dr. Smith because he/she is from Massachusetts, and I'm originally from Massachusetts."* Now this is a horrible basis upon which to choose a dentist, yet it's a realistic model your patients are using to make their decisions.

Working this point into your marketing subtly is a powerful "dog-whistle" that will call out to and attract the right patients, and this is only one, tangible example! Don't loose site of the lesson here; this is injecting *affinity marketing* into your practice, which is the most powerful connection you can make with prospective patients. But you'll never get to this unless you ask patients and then implement it.

Plussing Your Video Marketing

Walt Disney was credited with coining the idea of "plussing" your efforts. He challenged his Disney Imagineers to find ways of plussing their creations; which is to say, what other ways can we leverage what we've already created for the maximum penetration, reach, communication, and return on investment?

How can you leverage making a video? I teach <u>33 different ways</u> to leverage a <u>single video testimonial</u>. One is to turn the video into an audio. My business is predominately about video communication, but I'm not so disillusioned by the medium to think that it's the right medium for everyone. In fact, the vast majority of people I've ever interviewed tell me they would gladly welcome an audio CD of a presentation so they could listen to it in their car traveling to and from work.

Virtually every video you make can be converted to an audio only format and sent along with its video counterpart or offered separately to your audience. Statistics show offering patients a choice on how to consume the information increases the probability of response. For example, if you send out physical DVD's, add an audio CD to the package. You double the odds of getting the patient to see and/or hear your presentation, and the increased conversions will more than pay for the added investment for the audio CD. Turn the audio of a video into a prerecorded telephone message for people to hear testimonials while on hold.

Real Media vs. Fake Media

I use the word "media", in the sense of a marketing tool, as a vehicle for reaching and communicating with perspective patients. A local non-profit organization in the Cleveland, Ohio area spent $250,000 to redo it's corporate website. After the makeover they can't track a single cent in donations or revenues as a direct result of the website makeover. I'm not suggesting that the makeover wasn't needed or that websites aren't needed rather, you should carefully choose the media you employ, based on your buying audience. What media resonates best with YOUR patients?

Print & Direct Mail is real media – 54% of postcards mailed are read by recipients; 3.3 billion direct mail coupons were redeemed in

2010, 45% of consumers purchased from mailed catalogues, and 22-24 year olds are more likely to respond to a mail piece than other direct sales media (Direct Marketing Association Statistical Fact Book 2012).

For example, on a recent project I launched for a private dental client, I wrote a print advertorial for placement in her local newspapers.

The article promotes a unique service she offers and directs readers to call the practice (the scripted presentation converts callers to appointments with the dentist) or to visit a website to see a free informational video. Through both call tracking and web analytics we can measure calls and traffic to the video. With 2 concurrent runs of the ad it generated 11 new patient appointments, a 100% conversion rate , immediately added $44,000 annual revenue to the practice and a projected lifetime value of $220,000; just on revenue created by those 11 new patients and their immediate family.

Radio is real media – Radio can target the specific demographics of your audience and are rabid followers of specific programs and on-air personalities. You can reach and measure response quickly.

Television is real media – studies have shown that the average American watches approximately 125 hours of television a month (Comscore). An increasing number are consuming it online at YouTube. As of this writing, an Australian skydiver and daredevil managed to wrangle Red Bull as a corporate sponsor of his "jump from space" stunt wherein he broke both the highest free fall record and broke the sound barrier in free fall. The event drew over 8 million viewers to the live YouTube stream. There were a lot of key marketing factors in play here, but the one to note is people will rabidly consume video (and video is television).

Real media, by my definition, is media that can carry and convey your marketing message to a target audience and convert them to buying patients. Print/Direct Mail, Radio and Television are real media.

By my definition then, social media (Facebook, Twitter, etc.), as a whole, is fake media. It can however be effectively incorporated into a marketing campaign as strategy, but rarely do I see it generate any real revenue on its own. Perry Marshall, author of the book, ***"The Ultimate Guide to Facebook Advertising"*** (with whom I've worked and recorded on many occasions) states, "*People go to Facebook to avoid making decisions.*"

People use social media as an adjunct to real media.

In Chapter 18 you'll hear a 'real' media buyer (whom I work closely with) defines how to buy and use real media.

A TANGIBLE LESSON WITH YOUR TEAM

I hear 2 complaints about scripts; people don't like them because they make a person too robotic and not natural; and second, they're too long. First, the language is important because as I pointed out already, there's a lot of psychology at work and second, the script should be learned, memorized and practiced, just like developing skills as a hygienist or dental assistant, it's a learned skill.

And lastly, the script takes longer to read than it does to deliver in natural conversation. But, if your team is holding hard and fast to not wanting to use my sample script (from the resource site) because it's 'too long' (a case of the tail wagging the dog), then you'll also find a condensed version on the resource site as well.

Refer to the resource website to this book for a lesson to share with your team on asking for patient video testimonials. Go to www.BookOnTestimonials.com for access to the lesson.

Chapter 11

Your Key Differentiators

"You're not paid for what you know, you're paid for who you are and what you can do." Napoleon Hill (Author of the Best Selling Business Book, "Think and Grow Rich")

Who am I and why should you listen to what I'm about to share with you. I'm not a dentist so how could I know anything about marketing a dental practice? You're right, I don't know anything about marketing a dental practice, but I do know how to market people, because it's how I've grown my business. I'll let you in on a little secret. I don't spend one dime on traditional marketing, yet I have some of the country's most influential entrepreneurs as private clients; business people from different industries, including dentistry. People like Jerry Jones, Dr. James McAnally, Dr. Tom Orent, Dr. Chris Griffin and Dan Kennedy (a leading marketing strategist to dentists for the past 40 years – DanKennedy.com), not to mention dozens of solo-docs just like you, who you'll come to meet in the following paragraphs.

My journey in helping dentists started with my own family dentist, Dr. Manbir Pannu in North Royalton, Ohio. Manbir is a retired Lieutenant Colonel from the US Army. She served troops during Operation Iraqi Freedom. She's a great person, a fabulous GP and passionate about her practice and patients (sound familiar?). With 2 operatories, running the practice, doing all the dentistry herself, including cleanings, she

Manbir Pannu, DDS

struggled to grow her practice. She has advocate patients, a solid practice and up-to-date dental equipment, but struggled to expand it. I offered to help and the one strategy (actually two, but interpreted by patients as one) that I'll share with you here brought more new patients in one month than any month in practice history. Don't misunderstand me, I know nothing about the science behind dentistry, however I know what patients want and I know how to give it to them in the marketing message.

I'll tip my hat a bit here; Dr. Pannu had all the right elements of her story to share with patients, but she wasn't using it in her marketing at all. In her marketing, she was selling teeth whitening, free exams, free consultations and discounts; like so many other dentists advertising to the same group of patients.

 What elements did she posses, but wasn't using? Two: her personal story, and letting advocate patients share their stories about being a patient in her practice. I'm talking about story telling and patient testimonials. I don't have enough space here to discuss the true power behind story telling in marketing and it won't be my focus here, but if you've followed Jerry Jones long enough and have studied his style of dental practice marketing, you already understand it. As for patient testimonials, that's my specialty, and most every dentist I meet and talk with understands that patient testimonials are valuable to have in their marketing, yet most struggle to get them, and those that do have them aren't squeezing every last ounce of equity out of them that they could.

Recently, my friend and fellow mastermind member Stephen said to me *"last week I attended my dentists' funeral"*. He shared this with me, knowing that I work with dentists. Stephen told me that he'd gone to high school with his dentist and as far as he knew, he and his practice were doing well. Not until attending the funeral did Stephan discover that his high school pal had been struggling to keep his practice afloat financially. Stephan told me that he was a good man, a great dentist and civic leader in the community. It came as a shock to him when this pillar of society felt the only way out was to take his own life.

Unfortunately it's a staggering statistic among dentists. Plus, dentistry is continuing to change; if you don't think so, read Jerry Jones' full report entitled ***"The State of Dentistry"*** (http://thestateofdentistry.com/). It conveys a very true picture of where dentistry is headed for the solo-practitioner. Of the docs I have as private clients, I see vast similarities in them. They all started a practice to serve their patients, to be the best dentist they could be; and to provide a good life for their families. I've seen a common core principle that every successful doc understands and leverages in their practice. It's the primary thing most every patient is looking for in their dentist; at least as told to me by the hundreds of dental patients I've interviewed over the years; and it's at the foundation of the marketing tool I'll reveal in this chapter. It's the one thing no dentist establishes early enough in the relationship with his or her patients. It's something that develops naturally between the doc and patient, though it can be accelerated to the point of eliminating fee resistance when it's established properly. I'll share actual case examples later in the chapter, from real patients, patients who I've personally interviewed and have told me in their own words.

You too may be a dentist who's tried to implement a system for getting testimonials from patients, yet struggled to make it work. By the time you're done reading this chapter you'll understand not only how to get a testimonial, but what a great one looks and sounds like. I'll reveal the techniques and strategies I've developed; the ones my private patients hire me to do and implement for them.

Chapter 12

HOW PATIENT TESTIMONIALS ARE INFLUENTIAL?

"No one cares what you know until they know how much you care." Zig Ziglar

I was taught to never assume that someone knows something, just because I myself know it. So, if you know what a testimonial is, bare with me. Simply put, a patient testimonial is social proof. It's another person speaking about their experience with you, your practice or your team and the results they gained from that relationship with you. You'll notice I wrote "their experience with you…". For the patient, it's all about the experience. At the time of this writing, 74% of the US population fears going to the dentist for one reason or another. This is a huge obstacle for you in attracting new patients, let alone getting them to accept the cases you present to them. My client Dr. Robert Matiasevich, in Santa Cruz, California sums up marketing his practice like this, *"The biggest challenge I face in marketing my practice, isn't getting the new patient to come into the practice, it's getting them to pick up the phone and call the practice."*

Dr. Bob Matiasevich
Santa Cruz Family
Dentistry

Robert Collier, a successful marketer and author of The Robert Collier Letter Book (published in 1937) wrote that the quickest way to connect with a prospect, in your case prospective patients, is to enter the conversation already going on in their mind. What are the conversations they're having with themselves, their spouse, friends or coworkers when they're looking for a dentist? 74% of them don't want to go to a dentist to start with and they have an even bigger problem changing dentists even when their experience with the existing dentist isn't good. The idea of changing dentists to look for another is more painful than enduring poor care from their present one. Picture that new patient who does overcome the fear and calls your practice. As they stand outside the door of your practice for the first time they unconsciously (or consciously) ask themselves, *"will my experience with this dentist be any different than my past dental experiences?"* In a moment you'll meet Shannon Wright, who asked herself that very question before she found her dentist, Dr. David Pearce (Baldwinsville Gentle Dentistry, Baldwinsville, New York), and one of my clients.

Dr. David Pearce
Baldwinsville Gentle
Dentistry

Before I show what a great patient testimonial feels like, it's helpful to understand your patient's mindset with regard to making a decision on which dentist to choose. The following is a transcript from an actual interview. Angela's comments reveal the struggle shared by so many patients when faced with picking a dentist for their care.

"I had received flyers in the mail from this practice I just stuck it into my pile and thought maybe when I go to the dentist I'll think about

Angela Stoutenger
Baldwinsville, NY

going to them, then I thought, you know it's really time, I really need to go to the dentist. I was really torn because another coworker was going to a different dentist in Baldwinsville and she had just started going to him and she had been having a good experience so I was really torn between the two but, I don't know, there was something about Dr. Pearce, I don't even remember if it was something about what they said and, I don't know, I just thought to myself, this is the dentist for me."

You see a patient testimonial can enter the conversation your prospective patients are having with themselves. In direct selling those conversations are called obstacles or objections. They're the things that keep a patient from picking up the phone and calling the practice. They're also the things that prevent the patient from accepting your treatment plan because unless you address and answer their objections, it's a struggle to convince a patient that the case you present, no matter the fee, is the right one for them. It comes down to trust. As a dentist you're in the trust business. To truly break the fee resistance barrier with patients they have to trust you.

There are 9 things that your patients are trying to figure out about you. Not until they're able to satisfy these 9 questions will trust be established between you. When you analyze the patients that you have now, those that accept your diagnosis and plans with little hesitation, you will find that they've already satisfied these 9 concerns. Once these 9 concerns are addressed and satisfied, you'll no longer be viewed by the patient as *a dentist peddling his/her services*, but rather a trusted dental advisor.

The 9 Things They Are Trying to Figure Out About You

1. **Authenticity** - Are you real? Or is the marketing just a bunch of hype?
2. **Believability** - Are you telling the truth?
3. **Credibility** - Are you knowledgeable and competent?
4. **Feasibility of the relationship** - Are you appropriate for them? Can they see themselves being comfortable with you?
5. **Customized solutions** - Are you listening to them or are they just a number in the practice?
6. **Safety/Security** - Are you reliable and can you be relied upon?
7. **Comfort** - Do they understand enough about what you can do for them
8. **Superiority** - Are they making the best choice versus other choices available?
9. **Value** - Are they paying a 'fair' fee?

* (The '9 Things' are borrowed from Dan Kennedy and can be read in greater detail in his No BS Trust-Based Marketing book – Amazon.com or B&N.com)

I won't go into detail on each of these because they're self-explanatory. I provide this merely for your understanding that prospective patients are judging you against these 9 fundamentals. As a consumer of products or services yourself, you're making these same determinations, consciously or subconsciously. Their importance increases proportionally as the investment for a product or service increases. Patient testimonials and the sharing of their experiences with you will significantly accelerate a new patient to draw a positive conclusion on these fundamentals. What others say about you is more effective, impactful and influential than what you would say on your own behalf. Napoleon Hill wrote *"They won't hear you until they know you"*. They won't trust you until they've figured out these 9 things about you and when they do, they'll feel they know you; when they know you, they'll hear you. They'll hear your case presentation from an open, non-adversarial position.

Without first having created and established trust, your case presentation will be heard through defensive guard. The patient will have their guard up. Think of a professional boxer who holds fists in front of his face to protect himself from the opponent's jabs and punches.

It's unavoidable, but every selling situation, including case presentations, creates an adversarial situation. Your patient in the role of the opponent, with hands rose to their face to protect themselves from jabs and punches is on guard for the 'price' of the dental case. Remember, most patients have had poor experiences with well intentioned, but ignorant dentists; their words not mine. There are 2 things I hear consistently from patients I interview 1- they felt treated only as a number on a medical chart and 2- they felt the doctor recommended dental work only to 'up the bill'! These are the obstacles you're facing, whether they tell you or not you must recognize it. Testimonials are a powerful tool to dismay these beliefs and cut through past dental 'baggage'.

Having and using patient testimonials allows prospective patients to hear from people just like themselves, who have already experienced what they themselves will experience. It gives your prospective patient a model against which to decide if you are right for them (#4 from the list), are you reliable (#6), have you heard their concerns and addressed it in you're dental plan (#5) and is the value greater than the fee paid in exchange for the plan (#9)?

Ron Sheetz

Chapter 13

TYPES OF PATIENT VIDEO TESTIMONIALS

There are 2 types of patient video testimonials; the *delivered* (or *survey*) testimonial, and the *interview* (or *documentary*) testimonial.

The Delivered Testimonial (Survey)

The delivered testimonial is the most common. A delivered testimonial is one where the patient usually stands before the video camera and talks extemporaneously. Without advanced coaching or guidance they often rattle off the first things that come to their mind. These are often well-intentioned comments, but are void of any marketable content. These testimonials typically reflect adoration for the doctor and/or staff. Here are transcripts from actual patient video testimonials captured by a dental team prior to my working in their practice and teaching them how to create powerful patient testimonials:

1) *"I came to this dental office today on an emergency basis and they got me in immediately. This is the friendliest dental office I've ever been in the years I've been alive."*

2) *"Every time I come into Dr. X's office the staff is great, they're friendly, the service is good and I enjoy coming back."*

3) *"This is my first visit to Dr. X Gentle Dentistry. The first experience was great. I felt very relaxed and very well taken care of and it was a pleasant experience."*

4) *"What I enjoyed about my first appointment was that the staff was very friendly, they answered all of my questions. They talked to me step by step through the process of what they were going to do and the dentist came in and rather than just checking my teeth and leaving he made sure he talked to me for a few minutes and addressed all of my issues and concerns that I had."*

You can see they speak highly of the doctor and practice; however these are 'feel-good' testimonials. There are 2 major components missing from these examples: the patient's backstory or what the catalyst for treatment was, and their final results. A patient's backstory is a powerful point of connection for prospective patients and the positive results are what every patient is interested in. You can tell from these examples they like the practice, but as a viewer I don't know what brought them to this doctor (backstory), what the doc did, and what the outcome was (results). These testimonials are too general. They'll leave a viewer (your prospective patient) thinking, *"that's nice, but it doesn't apply to me because my case is different"*. Without connecting your prospective patient to your existing patients (through experiences), the testimony has no validity for the prospective patient and therefore is perceived as just a glossy statement of approval.

People connect with other people because of shared stories or experiences. When I interview a patient, I'm always probing for their stories; what they went through that brought them to where they are today. Therein lies connection with other patients for your practice. If a prospective patient doesn't connect with the story then its just rhetoric, it's not effective marketing for you (it is through a patient's pain that a prospective patient will connect). I call this *Doctor Benefit by Proxy*. The prospective patient's mindset is; *"that patient is like me and Dr. X was able to help him or her so therefore, Doctor X can help me"*.

Now, with that understanding, most delivered testimonials would fall short as an effective marketing tool for your practice. There are some people who can nail it; they can give you a very content rich delivered testimonial. I've found these types of people to be very introspective. They're both emotionally and intellectually motivated. However, they're few and far between. I've reviewed thousands of delivered testimonials and when I hear them one after another after another after another, they all sound the same. This isn't the fault of the patient; they don't know what to say. Asking someone to give you a testimonial, puts them on the spot and in an awkward position. They won't know what to say, so they'll say what they think will be helpful to you. Unfortunately, it often times is not. With a little guidance as to what to say you can capture some great testimonials. The guidance you can provide them can be borrowed from the *interview testimonial*, which I'll cover next. Simply borrow the format I'll show you and give it to them as bullet points to follow when they give their testimonial.

The Interview Testimonial (Documentary)

The second type of testimonial is one captured by interviewing a patient, rather than letting them speak impromptu. Think of film or TV documentaries, they're in depth case studies on their subject. I developed my method of interviewing patients and creating detailed dental practice documentaries from studying hundreds and hundreds of feature film documentaries. It took me a long time to convince my accountant that the movie DVD's I bought were a business expense and should be classified under continued education (I love the films too, but that's a residual benefit).

My client Dan Kennedy is the most highly paid and sought after direct response copy writer in the world; so I think he knows a thing or two about influencing people through writing. In fact, he calls what he does as salesmanship in print. That's what you need to do, whether you like it or not, you need to influence people and sell them on your approach to their dental care as being the best approach for them (this goes back to the 9 fundamentals model; #5 – *customized solutions*). To simplify it, Mr. Kennedy often employs a "problem, agitate, solution" model in his writing. Pay attention here, you'll begin to see the similarities develop with what I wrote earlier. Presenting the backstory or problem first provides the point of connection and it's important to connect with prospective patients early; this is an engagement technique. Next, agitating the problem with their symptoms elevates the pain. It's like applying salt in an open wound. And finally, the solution obtained by following the same action as the subject in the story; your existing patient. This is a very effective selling model to follow.

Here's the model that I adapted from it and use for patient testimonials.

- Pain
- Agitate
- Turning point
- Solution

What is the patient's pain? It could be physical tooth pain or the life-long embarrassment of an unflattering smile; one they hide behind their hand every time they smile.

What was the turning point? What is the 'thing', the catalyst that finally motivated them past their fears to seek out a dentist to fix the problem? There's always one major thing. It's the 'thing' that finally clicked for them to take action! 74% of the US population fears the dentist. I've lost count of how many patients I've interviewed that told me of the 5, 10, 30 and 45-year hiatus they took from seeing a dentist. I also hear from patients how they endured well intentioned, but poor dental care because it was easier than finding a new dentist, not to mention their fear of entering a worse dental care situation than they were in already.

And then finally, what's the solution? For my private dental clients, the solution is always them and their practice. Through compelling patient interview testimonials, a prospective patient clearly sees the best solution; the only real solution is you! This is the model I employ. These are the components of a great testimonial!

Here's a transcript from another patient I interviewed and captured on video for a private client. You will be able to clearly identify the pain, turning point and solution model within this testimonial:

"I'm terrified of the dentist, terrified, like by terrified I mean cold sweet breaking out and running down my face.

It started way back when I was a little girl, I mean, I had a dentist pull a tooth, an impacted tooth, I was ten, and he said that I was being a baby. But he hadn't given me

Shannon Wright
Baldwinsville, NY

enough Novocain, and the next thing, what I remember is kicking him and running out and blood was running down my face and my mother was horrified.

Maybe I just picked the wrong dentists and I'm glad that I finally picked one that's a winner.

I was finally forced to find a dentist when the Anbosal and Tylenol would no longer make the pain go away from my tooth that was abscessed.

I cannot place a value on anything that Dr. Pearce has done with my dental work; I can't. It really has changed my life.

I smile more, I laugh more, I take more pictures, you know like family pictures.

I don't sit in the corner anymore. I talk to people. When you have really bad teeth you try to cover them and hide them. You become a master and an expert at it. I don't have to do that anymore; you know, I mean it's, now, I literally have the perfect smile, the perfect smile for me. Dr. Pearce was everything I needed him to be."

The 2 components that produce this testimonial were the questions I asked of the patient and how the final testimonial was edited for presentation.

But what questions do you ask a patient?

The questions are very subjective to your practice. If I were working with you to develop a powerful patient video testimonial library or documentary film about your practice, I'd ask you what obstacles or objections you encounter during case presentations; those that prevent patients from moving forward with your treatment plan? Simply formulate questions that address those objections and then ask your existing patients the right questions that lead them to answers that will overcome those objections.

The questions are the key. They're designed to elicit the kind of responses you must have. The questions by themselves are just questions, but in the hands of a skilled marketer they craft your message.

(You will find a list of questions I've developed at www.BookOnTestimonials.com)

How do you get patient testimonials?

When I speak before groups of dentists I ask for a show of hands of how many are actually getting video testimonials? Usually it's a third of the room—that's not bad. Then I ask how many find it a struggle to get them; or alternatively, docs who struggle with their teams to get them? Here's why.

I'll first approach it from your team's perspective. Your team is uncomfortable asking. They wouldn't be comfortable going on camera if asked therefore they're uncomfortable to ask others to do it.

They also feel awkward asking. These are two different things. I refer back to hygienist Donna Collins who shared with me during an interview *"The doctor wants us to get video testimonies, but I just feel icky asking."* Those were her exact words. "I feel icky." Questioning her further it was because she thought that asking her patients to go on video was outside the scope of the relationship she'd developed with her patients. When I showed her how to ask, it completely changed her mindset and comfort level, and she no longer felt icky asking. The problem was her mindset and approach was wrong.

Additionally your team may not understand what the real value of testimonials are and what they can mean for the practice. Then there's the fact that some people are "technologically challenged". They just don't like technology, or are intimidated by it.

From the patient perspective, they're shy; they don't like cameras. They don't like the way they look or sound on camera. They also don't know what to say. I described it earlier with the delivered testimonials. These testimonials often contain verbal vomit. No one likes being put on the spot. Without properly preparing a patient before asking them to give you a video testimonial, would be putting them in an unfamiliar and uncomfortable position. Their instinctive response will be fight or flight. They'll give you all kinds of reasons why they can't do it or they'll just say no. Either way you won't get a video testimonial, and asking patients incorrectly could potentially tarnish your relationship with that patient.

CHAPTER 14

LEVERAGING VIDEO TESTIMONIALS IN YOUR PRACTICE MARKETING

You can use the techniques and strategies I've shared with you to this point to capture only written testimonials, but you're doing yourself a disservice by not pursuing video testimonials. There are several advantages by having video testimonials over just a written one. Video is so effective because it is the closest form of communication to an in person conversation. There's tremendous power in being able to see a person's body language and hear the authenticity of emotion and feeling in a person's voice. A UCLA professor conducted a study on effective communication and found that 55% of the communication between people occurred in body language, gestures and facial expressions. 37% of the communication takes place in how a person says what they say, in their voice and tonality, and only 8% of the communication is in the actual words. So in having only a written testimonial, you're missing out on 92% of true power of communicating with prospective patients.

Another effective opportunity with video testimonials is that it can be applied in your marketing and advertising in 3 different mediums; video, audio, and print. A video testimonial is made up of video, audio, and words. You can insert testimonials in video form on your website, or playing on the big screen TV in your patient waiting area. You can extract the audio from the video and use an excerpt in a radio commercial, or on your website (hear an example at www.BookOnTestimonials.com). Have the audio portion of the video transcribed and use excerpts from it in print advertising. You also can lift a still frame captured from the video in picture form and apply it with the text version of the testimonial.

As of writing this book, I've identified 33 different ways a single video testimonial can be applied in any practice's marketing and advertising.

I share all 33 methods on the resource site at www.BookOnTestimoinials.com

Here are 3 examples of how I crafted different practice marketing pieces from the testimonials I captured for clients. Each of these examples are still being used by the practices to attract new patients yet today.

From Dr. Demetrakopulos' practice documentary, I extracted 90-seconds of patient testimonials and turned it into a commercial that runs on loop in the local cinema during the daily movie schedule. This application of patient testimonials in an out-of-category medium has provided Dr. Demetrakopulos' practice with a flood of new patients. We're applying what we already have in a medium where she's in a category of one, all by herself.

Other dentists can buy this kind of advertising space, but we're the first to use live video and actual patient testimonials in the advertising. Video and sound testimonials are more impactful than only print ones. They communicate the emotion and authenticity that a print one cannot.

I have also extracted the audio from a video and applied it in other mediums, such as on-hold phone messages, radio spots, etc.

Sarah
Cleveland Hts., Ohio

Telephone Interview

A Profile of One of America's Best Dentists – North Royalton, Ohio

Affordable dental care without dental insurance?

I've also had the audio transcribed for use in print mediums, to fill white space or as quotes in advertorials.

"She cares for me and my health and not just my money."
Angela V. - Brunswick, Ohio

Earlier I told you that I don't spend a dime on traditional marketing and advertising. The bulk of my marketing is done through referrals and testimonial marketing. I can tell you from experience in having interviewed so many dental patients and dentists, that a majority of your practice's new patients are coming from referrals and word of mouth marketing. The sad part is; referrals are the easiest to systemize, yet the most under utilized marketing tool in most practices! When a patient tells me they've referred others to their dentist, I always ask if they know if that person ever followed through to contact the practice or became a patient. The typical response is, "I don't know", hence the absence of a system to generate and track referred patients.

The patient referral system I created relies on patient testimonials and is at the core of my Preferred Patient Duplication System™.

Chapter 15

THE FASTEST PATH TO CASE ACCEPTANCE

You face 2 major challenges from a business perspective; getting new patients to the practice, and getting those patients to accept the cases your present. In the following pages, I'll show you how to apply video testimonial marketing into your new patient process or funnel. This is a simplification of the process a new patient will experience when coming to a practice for the first time. Focus on the principles not necessarily the process.

A new patient can come to your practice through various sources, such as; referrals, word of mouth, television, radio, display ads, direct mail, newsletters, billboards, etc. Regardless of how the patient finds you, video testimonials can elevate and differentiate your position in the prospective patient's mind over competing dentists in your area. Seeing a dentist is not high on the list of things that people love to do. Remember Dr. Matiasevich's statement earlier? *"My biggest marketing challenge is not to get the patient in for an appointment; it's getting them to pick up the phone and call to make an appointment."* It's becoming more difficult to motivate patients to call your practice. There are now big corporate practices offering cheap dentistry; selling their services mostly on low prices, ultimately devaluing and commoditizing dentistry. Traditional methods of getting patients are becoming obsolete and ineffective. I see very little dental advertising and marketing that include patient testimonials, let alone any full-blown testimonial marketing; marketing made up entirely of testimonials. Traditional marketing relies on promoting an offer or opportunity such as an introductory exam or cleaning. Much of today's dental marketing is geared at promoting the deliverable, rather than promoting the results, let alone the doctor.

During our interview together, Dr. Zan Beaver, First Coast Family Dental, shared with me that in measuring traffic to his  website, he found people spent 63% more time at the *"meet the doctor"* and *"meet the staff pages"*. Not only are they the most visited pages, they're also the pages people stay engaged on longest. Patients tell me that when visiting a doctor's website, seeing a picture of the doctor and learning more about him or her is comforting, and has a major

Dr. Zan Beaver
First Coast Family Dental

influence on whether they call the doc or not. Most make a decision whether they like the doctor...or not, based on his or her picture and story. Imagine how much more powerful this could be if your site included a short "Meet the Doctor" video where they get to hear and actually meet you, along with patient testimonials adding credibility to your marketing?

For your patient, their satisfaction with you and your practice depends on 2 critical factors; your skill as a dentist, and your chair side manner. They need to know, like, and trust you. You can have the best skills in the world, but if you don't have a great, or even a good chair side manner, you're not going to develop long-term patients. There are only 2 ways a patient can determine whether they like you and ultimately trust you; through referral, and actually meeting you.

For the patient it's all about the experience and all too often, their true experience with you doesn't begin until they come into the practice. Sure, they can talk to your receptionist on the phone and they can check out your website, but the true measure is when they step through your door and experience it for themselves. Only then will they really know what it's like to be a patient in your practice. Video testimonials are a pivotal component in positioning you and your practice in the mind of the patient, and it can have a significant effect on whether a patient follows through with a visit and more importantly, proceeds with the case you present and at your fee. Here's a general look at the average new patient practice funnel:

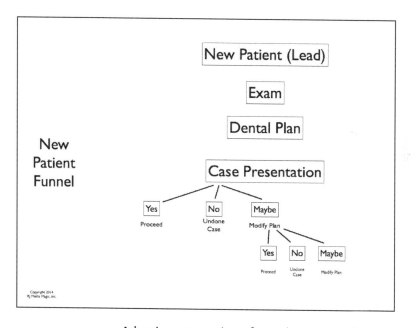

A basic new patient funnel

The patient enters the practice and gets an initial exam. From the exam you identify opportunities for dental work. I see dentists who create long-term strategies of the plan being implemented over a period of time, and those that offer good-better-best alternative plans from which the patient can choose.

In either event once the plan is developed the case is presented. In direct selling we call this the sales conversation. It's the dreaded uncomfortable part for doctor and patient in this newly forming relationship... it's where you get to talk price. I find few doctors like presenting the price and even fewer patients like hearing it, but it's an inevitable part of the relationship; and the key word here is <u>relationship</u>. You want to establish a relationship with your patient as early as possible. Too often the money gets in the way. Why? If you're getting sticker shock from the patient when you present the fees for a case, it's because you haven't created enough value to offset the fee. Fee resistance is when the fee is higher than the value the patient receives in exchange for the fee. Recently I interviewed Jeff Wiebe a patient of Dr. Steve Garrett, Hillsborough Family Dentistry, in Hillsborough North Carolina. Mr. Wiebe told me that Dr. Garrett

Jeff Wiebe
Hillsboro, NC

recommended that he needed a 2 tooth bridge and that it would cost $3800. I asked Jeff if he'd sought a second opinion or quote on the diagnosis? He told me no and when I asked why not, his reply was, "*He's my dentist and I trust him.*" This is where you want to be with every patient in every case presentation. The value of what the patient receives must far out weigh the fee the patient will invest in the dentistry. When achieved this will eliminate fee resistance. How do you accomplish this? Start the patient's experience with you sooner in the relationship. The following model illustrates where you can apply video testimonials to accomplish this. You'll see that I'm working on developing the value of their relationship with you sooner and more frequently than typical.

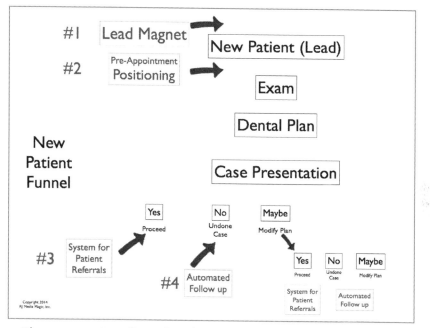

The new patient funnel with patient testimonials insert in to the practice's communication with patients to speed rapport and relationship building

#1 – A DVD of your patient video testimonials can be used as a piece that prospective patients can request. This is called a lead magnet. The concept is that rather than attract patients through traditional offers (free exams, free x-rays, etc.) you advertise to send patients a DVD offering them the opportunity to experience what it's like to be a patient of your practice. Patients would call the practice or go online to request to have the DVD sent to them in exchange for sharing their mailing address with you, hence the capture of a lead. The travel industry has employed this marketing strategy successfully for many years. Understand that it does delay the patient actually contacting your practice to schedule an appointment though there is great benefit in delaying the appointment. By building value and rapport first you're working on developing the relationship before you start selling dentistry.

Unlike traditional advertising, it sends a different message to prospective patients. Where as traditional advertising and offers communicate that a case presentation (sales pitch for dentistry) will likely ensue, offering a DVD and giving the prospective patient the chance to check you out sends an entirely different message. I've gained many clients through this method of marketing. It's both the delayed sale and a bit of take away selling. Traditional advertising telegraphs that you want their business, it communicates that you're going to sell something, just as every other dentist's advertising communicates. Offering them information about you, which they're going to investigate anyway, actually speeds your ability to build rapport with them. This form of advertising communicates, *"We're here and we're in no hurry to sell you. Check us out and decide for yourself if we're right for you. If we are, we'd love to see you, if we're not, no harm, no foul."*

This is very similar to referral marketing. When an existing advocate patient refers someone to you, the new patient is at a more advanced stage in their buying process than the patient who comes to you through traditional advertising. We call that the difference between a warm and cold lead. The new patient's experience should begin long before they call or visit your practice. No one likes to be 'sold', but everyone loves to buy something they seek. A DVD of testimonials, or a documentary film about your practice, offers prospective patients the opportunity to see and hear what it's like to be a patient in your practice before they ever have to commit to picking up the phone and scheduling that first appointment.

#2 – When a patient comes to the practice through a traditional form of marketing or advertising, they can be mailed your DVD of patient testimonials before their first appointment (when time allows – but you can control this). Most patient's first impression of a dental practice is on their first call or visit to the office. This is what every other dentist does and you don't want to be like every other dentist. You must get a jump on it. Don't allow the patient experience to just happen, control it. How much more receptive do you think a patient would be to your case presentation and fee if they enter the practice pre-qualified to expect a higher level of dentistry and care than they would from any other practice?

Two things will happen; you'll elevate the quality of the patients entering your practice, and you'll attract more of your ideal patients. You'll also repel a certain percentage of prospective patients. This isn't a bad thing. Those patients who request, receive, and watch your patient testimonial DVD or practice documentary film and conclude that you're the dentist for them, will come to your practice better prepared and predisposed to accept the treatment plans you present to them.

Sending this type of information, you'll have invested only a few dollars for the DVD and shipping, and saved valuable time you would have wasted on an exam. There's nothing worse than taking the time to develop and present a treatment plan, only to have the patients say no; not to mention the cost and time to you for your staff to process the patient and paperwork.

#3 – For patients who have the propensity to refer you, a patient testimonial DVD or documentary film can create the systematized referral process I spoke of earlier. The traditional referral tool I see practices using is a business card, because they're cheap and easy to hand out. Patients can be instructed to give them away to friends, family members, or coworkers and puts your contact information in their hands, but what ultimately happens to those business cards? Business cards are small and easily lost or forgotten.

Instead, provide patients with a properly packaged testimonial DVD they can hand out. This is an example of the type of documentary films I produce for private clients. Depending on the quantity, these can be reproduced for a little more than a dollar and they have a greater perceived value than a business card, plus they're harder for patients to throw away or lose. Unlike a business card, your DVD

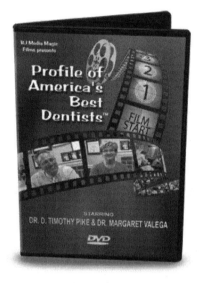

can actually tell your story and is an excellent way to start the relationship with a perspective patient; not to mention positioning you very differently from other dentists. *Perception is reality.* Additionally, your patient, the person referring you and passing on the DVD, doesn't have to be a great salesperson. All they need to do is give away the DVDs for you. I provide my clients with a very simple one-liner they teach patients when giving away the DVDs. Including some type of offer or bounce-back inside the DVD allows you to then track referral activity.

Not too long after completing the documentary film about their practice, one of my clients purchased a second practice. We leveraged the film a step further by sending patients in the acquired practice a DVD introducing him or her to their new dentists. The objective was to minimize patient attrition during the transition, as well as elevate the patient's expectation for the new docs. So far it's proved very effective. The new practice is already showing growth under the new owners.

#4 – What about those patients that don't proceed with a case? What do they do? What do you do? There's money in the follow up in undone cases. Too often I see practices that don't follow up on patients who took the time and effort to come in for an exam, get a dental plan worked up, hear the case presentation and then don't proceed. With these patients, you've already invested in them through your marketing and advertising dollars, and in the time to see them on the initial exam. Why would you want to leave money on the table and let cases go undone? Those patients that don't proceed with your case are either going to find another doctor and proceed with their case, or, the more likely thing to happen, is they'll do nothing. These patients still have the need and it's not likely that need is going away any time soon. Why not continually follow up with them? Not with aggressive marketing, but by building value. One of the most renowned sales trainers, Zig Ziglar, used to teach that people who initially say no to a case they later say yes to. They didn't change their mind about the case, but rather made a new decision based on new information. There's no telling why a patient may turn down your case, but they may say yes at a different time. You would never abandon a patient in need; why would you abandon a prospective patient in need? You'd be doing that patient a disservice.

Patient video testimonials can be formatted and applied into an automated email follow up campaign and depending on how detailed you want to get, the testimonials selected for the campaign can be targeted toward the needs of each patient. For example, a prospect who comes to you for orthodontics can receive only those patients you've performed orthodontics on, or a prospect who needs implants will hear only from your implant patients, etc. These sequences can easily be set up and launched automatically. It can be a "set it and forget it" campaign that continually works in the background to turn those 'no' prospects into 'yes' patients. Best of all, these types of automated sequences can cost little to no money depending on your existing systems.

I've just given you 4 ways to apply patient video testimonials into your new patient funnel in its native video form. Go back and review my list of 33 ways to leverage a single video testimonials in your marketing (www.BookOnTestimonials.com) as a whole and in a very short time, with little effort and some imagination, you can start interjecting patient testimonials in all your communications.

Leonard Bernard Shaw wrote, *"The problem with communication is the illusion that it's taken place."* Which is to say, just because you know something to be true, doesn't mean that others will know it as you have. Never underestimate the power of communicating with your patients and prospective patients with patient video testimonials. With very little effort, time, and investment you can significantly improve the quality and effectiveness of your marketing, advertising, and communications to people not yet a patient in your practice.

Chapter 16

Using Video to Leverage Your Affinity, Authority, Expertise and Celebrity

Answering the question, *"what makes you and your practice different"* can be a monumental challenge for anyone. You take for granted what you do when it's the 'thing' that your patients will easily identify as your differentiator. Most of you are guilty of underestimating your true value; meaning your not charging enough for our services.

With the proliferation of large dental practices and franchised/corporate run dental mills, there are 2 things you posses that these behemoth practices can't claim and unless you capitalize on them you'll continue to compete with these practices on price, and they'll continue to outspend you in advertising. The 2 things that you can leverage and they can't, is your story and your reputation.

In previous chapters, I described several tactical ways to differentiate your practice from competition. In this chapter I'll give you 5 specific video marketing strategies. I've implemented each of these into my private dental client's practices.

Welcome to Our Home

A client of mine in the industrial manufacturing industry, Noshok, is a broker of pressure measuring and control devices. From their earliest days in a 4000 square foot manufacturing building, whenever I'd visit Jim Cole (CEO), he would take me on a tour of the facility. Even after he built a 38,000 square foot world headquarters, Jim took everyone on a guided tour of the facility. The tour was always fresh with new stories of specific products, clients, or exotic applications their products were being incorporated into. I once commented that his tour was similar to the guided tours I've taken at Walt Disney. Jim confided that he scripted the tours and everyone got the tour. His role was to show off the company, and made sure that every visitor understood what they did, and more importantly, what made them better than other brokers, and their products.

As a former performing professional magician, I have a lot of antique magic and memorabilia from famous magicians in our home. My office is also in our home, and I'm always working on new and interesting projects. We're also proud of our 2 children and their accomplishments, so when guests come to visit I take them on a tour of our home and share the 'stories'. When I visit a client's business for the first time I often get the tour. We do this instinctively, showing off what we're proud of, but why don't more businesses do this on the home page of their website?

Your website is your home for virtual visitors. Offering visitors a virtual tour of your practice is an inviting way to engage visitors and show off your practice. In addition to a tour of your practice, make it easier on the visitor to give them a tour of your website; what they'll find there, what will be of interest to them. Website surfer's attention span is that of a gnat. If they can't find what they're looking for within seconds, they'll click away and be on to the next site. In the days of *Yellow Pages* advertising, my first mentor taught me that people would start their search at the "A's", and call vendors one at a time searching for the solution to their problem. They'd keep calling until they found someone who could help solve their problem. The same is true with web surfers.

They'll keep looking until they find what they want. A welcome/tour video will immediately engage a visitor and allow you the opportunity to build rapport with them.

Know-Like-Trust

Patients are looking to connect with their dentist on a personal level. Patients want to know, like, and trust their dentist and the dental team. I shared that Dr. Zan Beaver measures and tracks every aspect of his marketing. Measuring his online analytics he found that visitors to his website hit the "*Meet the Staff*" page more than any other page on the site. They also spend more time on that page than any other. Why? They want to get to know the people that will be treating them.

Create a video interview with everyone on the team and give prospective patients the chance to meet the doctors and staff. You and your team can share your stories and 'reason why' you've chosen this profession. To patients, what goes on inside your practice is a scary and mysterious thing. Open your doors via your website and let people in. Here's a short list of elements you should include in your story videos.

- Personal stories
- Likes, family, hobbies
- Experience and training
- Personal and practice philosophies
- Articulate your uniqueness (each team member will offer their perspective)
- Involvement in the community
- Share your favorite patient stories and results
- Demonstrate your progress
- Talk about others on the team and their contributions

Remember, patients perceive video as an entertainment medium, and when you and your team appear on video you are, in a sense, performing. This is an opportunity to share your stories with a much larger audience without effort. We're all riding in boats that are getting faster and faster. We have more to do, and less time in which to do it. Video is a medium that lets you multiply your time; being able to reach more people with a one on one feel. It's the second best way to engage prospective patients and build rapport.

FAQ – SAQ

I've stated already, when the only element prospective patients have to compare dentists on is price then that's all they'll consider. Many patients don't know what questions they should ask. I see many websites offering those *"frequently asked questions"* in text form, but few present them in video. Sharing the answers to these FAQ's is another opportunity to build rapport with your visitors. A more advanced strategy is adding SAQ's or *"should ask questions"*. These are the really important questions patient should ask, but may not know to ask. Patients often pick up the FAQ's from conversations with family or friends and what they glean from the Internet. SAQ's are an opportunity for you to feature unique selling propositions within your practice. Offering questions that only <u>you</u> can answer will create differentiation from other practices. Remember, we need to connect with patient's hot buttons.

Patient Testimonials

This is your opportunity to share your patient's experiences with you and your practice. It's the ultimate leverage of affinity marketing connecting your existing patients with prospective patients through their shared situations and experiences. Their stories are authentic, and you should use as many of them as you can to build a preponderance of proof and credibility that what you promote in your marketing and advertising is true. There's no more powerful marketing tool than capturing and sharing your patient's testimony.

The Documentary

Matt Zagula, a financial advisor and client uses Internet marketing very successfully in his practice. However he incorporates other mediums in his marketing, such as direct mail, radio and television advertising, and live seminars. His views on Internet marketing are very astute and should be understood by more businesses. Matt speaks of the "Google Slap", which is being found online in a crowded space by distracted prospects. Think about your own Internet searches. You're looking for a solution and a simple Google search presents hundreds, even thousands of possible solutions. You have to choose. As you read through the sites you have more and more answers, not necessarily the ones you're looking for, and that usually creates more questions. So you keep searching for more answers, and now you become more confused by what you've stumbled across. So you continue searching and reading, only to find more information, getting more confused, and more distracted from the objective that brought you there in the first place.

When you compete in an environment with all your competitors, on or offline, you become a victim of the Google Slap, as Matt defines it. You want to market to your prospective patients in a vacuum, where your competitors aren't, and patients can't be allowed to make erroneous decisions. One of my favorite companies is Disney. My family are avid fans and we visit Orlando frequently. I enjoy it for two reasons; 1) the experience and 2) the chance to study their marketing. I mentioned marketing to your prospective patients in a vacuum. What that means is being able to control all aspects of your communication with them, and in a way that your competitors can't intrude on or disrupt. If you've ever been to Walt Disney World and been on any one of their rides, for example Pirates of the Caribbean, you know that your every experience on the ride is controlled. You're shuttled through a preshow preparing you for the story and ride. You're then loaded on a car that rides along a track, guiding you through the story, turning you to see what they want you to see when they want you to see it, hear it, smell it, and experience it. And when the ride ends, you're dropped off in a gift shop with no direct exit without having to pass by merchandise. Disney controls your every experience within their parks. You too should build a system to control your prospective patient's experience with you; preparing them for your first consultation meeting, and getting them into a state of mind predetermined to hear and accept your case presentation.

The Ultimate Dental Marketing

The ultimate video marketing strategy is to bring all 4 of the previous strategies I've mentioned in this chapter, into one program. I've mentioned in previous chapters having shot documentary films of my private client's practices. My particular presentation of this strategy is in a long-format television program titled *"Profile of America's Best Dentists™"* A 30-minute documentary television film that features you the dentist, your team, and patients all to tell the story that is your practice; what makes it different and why so many patients become advocates of your practice, singing it's praises. Leveraging all the strategies I've described into a television film creates powerful authority, celebrity, and expertise. It's a unique way to present one's self and practice unlike any other practice.

Because of the format and entertainment value of the film, it can be broadcast on television. The initial reaction I get when I suggest buying and broadcasting a 30-minute program on local television most immediate think it's going to be expensive. Actually it's the contrary. It can cost 10's to 100's of dollars per spot to buy a 30-second commercial spot on network and/or local cable television. Most people aren't aware of most local cable network's public access channels. Cable networks are required to provide their local areas with a predetermined amount of local access air time. Often this is used by local governments, school systems and churches, but it's available to anyone and the broadcast time on these channels can be owned for pennies on the dollar compared to traditional commercial spots.

Additionally, owning these blocks of broadcast time allow you to structure the content anyway you'd like, within reason. If you want to insert 3 commercial spots each lasting 2-minutes, you can do so. It's worth investigating in your local area. You'll be surprised how inexpensively you can own this kind of broadcast time. It's counter-intuitive, you can spend thousands of dollars for 30-second commercial spots on TV and only hundreds of dollars for 30-minute blocks of broadcast.

And yes, there are people watching these channels, even if you're not.

Beyond television, we use the same program as a direct mail marketing tool. By now you've surmised that the fundamental difference in my marketing strategies is creating a unique advantage, based on the who (you and your practice) rather than the what (dentistry). During a live presentation at his 2011 Marketing & Moneymaking Super Conference, Dan Kennedy

(DanKennedy.com) stated, *"We really hurt ourselves by getting focused on the product or service we sell and thinking that people are trying to find the best choice of that product or service. What they're trying to do is much more elemental than that, they're trying to find that go-to guy or gal; the guy or gal who will take care of their problem."*

You are the unique advantage that differentiates your practice from every other.

A unique application I applied for Drs. Pike and Valega in Poolesville, Maryland with their documentary film, was when they bought a second practice. The traditional course in taking over an existing practice is to send a letter to patients of the practice communicating the transition. I took a less than traditional approach. I wrote a cover letter to the patients of the practice with a message targeted at communicating how different (better) the docs taking over the practice were, and we demonstrated it by including a DVD copy of their documentary to the top 1000 active patients in the practice.

Pallet of Pike and Valega documentary DVDs waiting to be mailed to patients

After this introduction mailing, we held a meet and greet party for patients and docs. The film created tremendous personal connection with Pike & Valega. Patients were anxious to meet their new "celebrity" dentists. The results significantly outweighed the small per DVD investment in tying patients to the docs and retaining them in the practice.

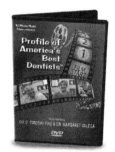 It's a powerful advantage so many people misunderstand, never consider and completely overlook... the power of celebrity. In the application I'm describing here, my branded and trademarked "Profile of America's Best Dentists" documentary film. Don't discount the power of this. Patients will instantly recognize it, identify with it and tell others. And when they're referring, it's a very strong position for you to be in; the celebrity dentist.

During my interviews with patients when filming the documentaries patients will often articulate it without me ever asking.

Kathy Wright is a patient of Dr. Pauline Demetrakopulos and shared this...

Kathy Wright
St. Helena, CA

"When I tell friends my dentist is recognized as one of the best dentists in America it gets their attention. Now it's not that Kathy had her teeth capped and they look great, it's now they were capped by someone who really knows what they're doing. Then they want to know where she is and if she's accepting new patients. And rather than giving out Dr. Pauline's business cards I hand them a copy of Dr. P's documentary film."

"Your expertise in creating a documentary of my practice, along with many patient testimonials, has given me a powerful tool to

use in my marketing. I can't thank you enough for the splendid work and for helping us to attract a wealth of new patients!"
Dr. Pauline Demetrakopulos – StHelenaDentist.com

"Video testimonials are perhaps the most powerful method to sway potential patients to the practice and Ron has a bullet proof technique for getting patients to happily give powerful testimonials. If you are looking to direct the growth of your practice in this new age, you should include Ron's technique in your armamentarium."
Dr. David Pearce – BaldwinsvilleGentleDentist.com

Behind the scenes shots during the filming of Drs. Pike & Valega's "Profile of America's Best Dentists™" practice documentary

Yes this is a DVD-based documentary film positioned as a national television show, but don't miss the advantage this kind of media (this is real media) can bring you. Additionally, the show is formatted for, and can be broadcast on television or cable.

Additionally, shorter versions can be created out of it for traditional TV and radio spots (as demonstrated earlier with Dr. Demetrakopulos' film being used in local cinemas).

The next chapter will give you insight into the three biggest forms of mass media available to you for distribution of a program and/or content from such a marketing vehicle.

Ron Sheetz

Chapter 17

ONLINE REVIEWS ARE KING (RIGHT NOW)

Right now people are relying on the Internet to get the bulk of their knowledge and information. There's no surprise that along with it come people's dependence on what others say about a product or service to influence their ultimate decision on what they will buy, and what dentist they will choose. To understand the importance of this here are some stats to consider:

- 94% of new patients use online search to find a local dentist
- 70% of consumers use the Internet to make a purchasing decision (including which dentist to call)
- 61% of people are searching online using mobile devices
- And 59% of those doing mobile searches will visit the business, and
- 70% of consumers trust businesses that have 6-10 positive reviews online
- 72% of consumers trust reviews as much as personal recommendations, and
- 90% of online searchers will take some action from their search within 24 hours

As reported by Neilsen, Google and Comscore

I've been seeing conversation that *"testimonials are dead"*, you should *"stop using testimonials and start getting and using reviews"*. I want to be clear, <u>testimonials</u> <u>are</u> <u>reviews</u>. It's just new lipstick on the same old pig. Everything I've shared with you up to this point about testimonials applies to reviews. Regardless of what you want to call them, testimonials or reviews, you should have them and be using them. For the sake of discussion in this chapter,

I'll refer to testimonials as reviews.

The Direct Correlation

There is a direct relationship between reviews and prospects. Presently online reviews are ranked from 1 to 5 stars, 5 stars being the best, and people are automatically conditioned to look at people or products with 4 and 5 stars. With that said reviews below 4 stars aren't worth looking at, because people are drawn to what they think is the best. Based on this rating system then 5 stars is the best. For the most part the rating system works, but it is flawed in that you can be subject to people posting bogus and inaccurate reviews about you.

There are 3-types of reviews:

1. A bad review
2. No review
3. Good reviews

Bad reviews are unavoidable, you're going to get them. With bad reviews, in many cases, you have the opportunity to respond to these, and should. A bad review should never go without a response from you. Your response to them should be calculated and positioned in a way that it opens the door for conversation between you and the disgruntled person leaving the review. Regardless of whether you and the party ever resolve the alleged issue, it's important that others reading the review and your response to it, and know you've acknowledged it and are interested in resolving it. Not responding to a poor review can give others the appearance that you're not interested in good patient service or don't want to acknowledge it.

A good review goes without speaking. As you've read about to this point, testimonials are not created equal and the same is true for reviews. I'll show you examples of reviews left about my family's dentist later and you'll see that most of them have a 'so-what' factor, which is to say they're a good review, but they have no influential value... and can easily be dismissed with 'so-what'.

Lastly there are the 'no reviews'. These are actually worse than a bad review. Remember, the majority of what is communicated is not in the written word. In the case of a practice that has no reviews, it says to a person, this practice isn't worth reviewing and will immediately be overlooked by someone searching and researching a practice online, and interested about other's experience with you. The ultimate result of no reviews is no calls to the practice. More detrimental to your schedule is the person who has made an appointment with you and then goes online to research you. Should they happen upon your name online and find you have no reviews they'll be more apt to cancel their appointment with you. At the same site they're likely to see your competitor's reviews, call their practice an schedule an appointment with them. All because you have no plan or system for getting and posting reviews for people to find them, where they're being found. It's easy to find prospects online, simply find out where they're looking and lay down in front of them (more on this later). You don't want to be the dentist with no reviews.

How Do People Search For Reviews Online?

You should understand people's online search behaviors, how are they finding reviews on you and your competitors? Most people follow a 3-step search process. I've learned this from asking patients who've found they're dentist online.

Regardless of the search engine used the following is a general illustration of most people's search behavior. Think about your own search habit. How do you find what you want, and once you find it what path do you follow online to learn more?

A General Search:

A patient wants to find out what dentists are in the area so they type *"dentist"* or *"dentist and the local city or town"*. It's not important to include the city or town in the search string because the search engines know geographically where they're searching from based on how your search engine is configured in the settings, plus by the IP address of the service provider. The general search returns potential dentists in the area; yours if you're doing the right S.E.O. (search engine optimization) stuff with your website.

Search by name:

Once the patient has a list of practices they search more information on the practices by searching the practice by name. This is in addition to visiting your site. People are instinctively cynical to the information on your site because you created it. They want '3rd party' insight on you.

Review search:

Next they'll search your name tagged with 'reviews', interested in what others have posted about their experience with you. All 3 of these searches are done through the traditional search engines, Google, Bing, Yahoo, etc. This is important to understand for what I will share next.

What You Must Know About Review Sites

Recently my wife had to see our family dentist because she chipped a tooth and had to get in to see Dr. Pannu quickly. She called the office and they got her in right away, as most good dentists will do with their patients. The appointment took only 10-minutes and my wife was thrilled, and made that comment. Because I've trained Dr. Pannu and her team to recognize 'testimonial triggers' she asked for a testimonial and Anne agreed to leave one.

Dr. Pannu has a system that sends an email to patients after every appointment. The email contained an active link to the review site. When my wife received the email later that night, after her appointment, she immediately left a review. The process was really an automated survey with the opportunity to leave comment, and it's the comment section that is what will appear on the review site. Had Dr. Pannu not gotten a verbal commitment from my wife to complete the review she might have not done so, by getting caught up in 'other things'.

That's a pretty normal process and pretty innocuous. Here's the problem most aren't aware of and the dental review services won't tell you. A few days after leaving the review of her experience with Dr. Pannu, at the site she was directed to via the active link, Anne wanted to see the review she left. She went to Google and typed "Dr. Pannu reviews" in the Google search. The first 3 results were to the website Yelp. The first to a Dr. Pannu in San Jose, California, the second to the Pannu Dental Group in Fremount, California and the 3rd the Pannu Dental Group in Cupertino, California. The next 4 choices lead to web pages that were not available and the last 3 to other Dr. Pannu sites, 2 of which were ranked review sites. None of the 10 search results on the first page of Google were the 'right' Dr. Pannu, in North Royalton, Ohio.

Not finding her review Anne went back to the email she'd received from Dr. Pannu's office and went directly to the site she left the review with; it was Rate-a-Dentist.com. Once on that site she searched for her review and found it immediately. So why didn't she find it on the open Google search? Because the site she'd left the review on, for Dr. Pannu, is not a ranked site. That means the site is not ranked well enough in the search engines to show up, even with a specific keyword search. Dental review sites, have the same challenge you have in getting your practice site ranked high enough in the search engines. You have an advantage these review sites don't, your search ranking is local whereas the review sites are competing nationally.

There are review sites that are ranked, such as Yelp, ZocDoc and Yellow Pages and those that are not. If you're reviews aren't posted on sites that are not ranked your reviews will never show up when patients in the 3rd step of their search behavior are searching for reviews about you specifically.

Here's the impact. Going back to my family dentist, Dr. Pannu (www.northroyaltondentist.com) and looking at the review site she has a contract with. Of the 10 docs listed on the local search only 2 have any reviews. Dr. Pannu was listed second on the page with 114 posted reviews and the doc listed first had 33 reviews and the remaining 8 had no reviews. Despite being second she'd be the first to be clicked on because of the number of reviews she has posted. That's excellent, but, those 114 reviews are useless to her because they don't show up on Google, Bing or Yahoo. All the effort Dr. Pannu is putting into getting patients to leave reviews is a waste of time and effort because despite doing a great job to amass a lot of reviews none of them are of any value because people searching for dentist reviews in North Royalton, Ohio are not finding her reviews.

The Quality of Reviews

Now, let's imagine you have a system for getting reviews and they are showing up on the ranked sites, so people searching you are finding your reviews. What's the quality of your reviews? The following are Dr. Pannu's posted reviews (reprint here with her permission)

Here's the first 10 of the 114 posted reviews.

Anne Sheetz
12/16/14
"I had gotten a small chip in my tooth and Dr. Pannu was able to get me in on such a short notice. They were able to work around my work schedule and fit me into their busy schedule with no problems. When I got there Dr. Pannu looked at my chip in my tooth, offered me various solutions in which all were solutions to correct my dental problem. We decided on a plan and I was in and out in about 10 minutes. I have been a patient of Dr. Pannu for many years. She knows my dental history and I trust her expertise."

Bernie Ferrini
12/8/14
"As always, pleasant, thorough and professional."

Kelly Kling
11/25/14
"Doctor Pannu and her staff are #1. They always take the time to listen to their patients and provide excellent care. If you FEAR the dentist...you definitely need to come in and see them. They will make you feel right at home....LITERALLY......I had a crown done today... and I was able to watch/listen to a movie and didn't even pay attention to what they were doing!!!"

Patricia Ray
11/19/14
"Excellent care and compassion....I always learn something new and feel confident that I have received the best care! Thank you and your staff!"

Andrea Williams
11/10/14
"Everyone was really friendly especially the dental hygienist. She was very personable and though this was my 1st visit, she made me feel as if I had been a patient for years."

Noel Jenkinson
11/1/14
"As usual my last visit was met with courtesy and quality service. I received excellent advice and was dealt with in a timely manner."

Trish 10/20/14
"Everyone in the office is friendly and helpful. The dentist is not my favorite place to go but at this

office they make sure it is a painless experience."

Valarie   Fendrick   *"I had my 6 month cleaning with Maureen. She is*
10/3/14   *very thorough and gives a lot of good advice!!*
                       Thanks for a great visit!!"

Mariah   Seither   *"LOVE the staff and the whole office."*
9/24/14

C. Rizen 9/22/14   *"My dental appointment was flawless - punctual,*
                       painless, professional and friendly. I was
                       continually impressed with the efficiency of
                       operations at the office of Dr. Pannu. The results
                       were excellent. The staff at this dental office go a
                       step beyond expectation and I would recommend
                       them to anyone. Well done!"

© RateABiz

If you read each the only that has a foundation of a story is Anne's (the first one); even it can be strengthened. The second has some foundation and both can be helpful in persuading a patient to call the practice. The other 8 however have what I call a 'so what' value. They lack connection between the patient posting the review and a prospective patient searching for you. The longest review listed here is 108 words. There's nothing that dictates how long a review can or should be. They should be as long as it takes to communicate the story and experience. Remember, the purpose of a review is to influence and persuade prospective patients to pick up the phone and call you.

Frequency & Recency

How many reviews are enough? It takes 5-10 reviews on ranked sites for your reviews to be positioned by the search engines. More important is having frequent and recent reviews. Despite it taking only 10 reviews to start showing up you must have recent reviews.

If you have 10 reviews dated from 2 years ago it communicates that no one's been happy with you since then. What people are saying about you today is more important than what they said about you 2 years ago, let alone last week. People looking for a dentist right now want to know what you're like right now.

Having frequent reviews communicates a preponderance of social proof, that people universally trust you, that you're safe. And a quantity of positive reviews communicates that you're consistent.

The 'Review-Target' That's Painted On Your Back

I was mentored in business during an era where it took years to build a reputation and only seconds to destroy it. Today a practice's reputation can be formed in 5-10 online reviews and a matter of seconds in the mind of a 'searcher'. As for reviews, your practice is dependent on the reputation they form about you, online, for searchers. Reviews are a form of referral and today's practices rely on referrals.

There are relationship liabilities you should be aware of, and concerned about when it comes to online reviews. As a doctor, you have a target painted on your back... or at least another. Having reviews available for prospective patients to find and use to decide whether you're the right dentist for them is valuable, until the reviews are negative, or worse yet, B.S.

The stats I shared at the start of this chapter tell you people are searching online and they're putting a great deal of credibility in what others post, however, people are more likely motivated to post a negative post than a positive. Think about your own experiences. If you have a good experience with a plumber for example, it can go without thinking because you expect to get good service. However, if the plumber is rude, arrogant, sloppy and inconsiderate in your home and after he's done he asks you to go online and leave a review about his service. You're pissed off about his behavior and how you were treated. You're anger is motivation enough to oblige his request. Doing this online is safe because you don't have to face the person so you can air your story, and often the emotion can cause the story be embellished upon, making it worse than it may have actually been.

On the other hand, if his service is excellent and he asks you to leave a review you may or may not get around to it; you're busy. You have every intention of getting to it, but life can get in the way and your attentions can get diverted elsewhere. It's human nature.

When you ask your patients to leave a review, even when you send them an email with a link and it will take only a few minutes, the same will happen to your patients, they'll put it off. Now, not all of them, but the majority of them will put it off and never 'get around to it'. You can't pin your hopes on patients following through.

The other problem is there's the potential for having negative posts left about you; from patients or people who aren't patients. Yes, it can happen; it's happened to my clients.

As a doctor, you have a target painted on your back for unanticipated and uncontrolled online reviews. People can and will denigrate you online. The Internet is an open forum were people can air their gripes and complaints publically, and until now there's little you could do about it. I mean, God forbid a patient feels they've gotten less than satisfactory service or care, or you didn't say hello to them in just the right tone when you walked into the operatory and they go online and post their hurt feelings for the world to see, hear and read. There's no stopping them. Worse yet, what about someone who's not even a patient posting some B.S.

review about you and your practice. That's right, someone you don't know and has never set foot in your practice posting about you. Think it can't happen, don't kid yourself.

You have only 2 recourses in fighting B.S. postings. One I mentioned earlier, the other is to hire an attorney and spend thousands of dollars to get those atrocious reviews removed from the Internet... hopefully. In some cases it can take months to make them go away... if it happened to you think about the damage they would do to your reputation.

It can shake you to your knees; not to mention the social impact it will have on you publically, and the irreparable damage it would have on relationships with your active patients. Slanderous? People are 'trigger-happy' to post their gripes and tell the world of how they were 'wronged'. And you, as the evil business owner and doctor, who's making buco-bucks (or so they think) don't stand a snowball's chance in the court of public opinion. Do you have the time, money or energy to fight the battle to get bad, untruthful reviews removed?

I don't think so

Instead mount a proactive campaign to get your patient's real stories and experiences with you and get those posted for the world to judge you by. If 72% of people trust online reviews as much as a personal recommendation then your reviews are not something you want to leave to chance and hope that your real patients will go online and post positive reviews about you. 'Hope' is not a strategy!

Go out and get your own reviews, real ones; ones that let people know what you're really like and let the public judge you based on reality, not someone hell-bent on settling a grudge. Don't be the victim, be the victor!

Reputation Marketing vs. Management

I said it earlier, your practice's success is dependent on it's reputation and reviews are presently the public's litmus for a practice's reputation based on other's experiences. "Reputation Management" or "Reputation Marketing"? Everything I've talked about in this book, as well as in this chapter on reviews is "Reputation Marketing". Marketing a positive reputation is something you do proactively, not something you hope happens organically. Truly successful businesses are grown through marketing, not management. During my days in corporate America, every business that worked at managing expenses struggled, and those focused on marketing and sales were successful. Sales make a successful practice, not savings.

You manage bad reviews, though you market a positive reputation. Reputation is something you create, not something that happens accidentally; or worse, believing that if you do a great job and are a great dentist that a good public reputation is automatic, or a result of being a hard worker. Your reputation is the only thing you can protect and you should protect it at all cost.

It requires 3 things to create powerful reputation marketing,

1. A plan for capturing powerful patient reviews (testimonials-what the bulk of this book has been about)
2. Crafting what is captured from patients and turning it into marketing material that clearly communicates your reputation
3. And a plan for implementing 1 & 2

Before you start you must know your starting point. What is your online-reputation based on reviews? Are your reviews being found and are your reviews influential and persuasive enough to motivate prospective patients to call your practice over the dentist down the street? Find out with a free Customer Review Report. You can access yours on the resource site at www.BookOnTestimonials.com

Ron Sheetz

Chapter 18

BUYING MEDIA – AN ENTREPRENEUR'S ULTIMATE CHALLENGE

Jessica Jones, *founder* | RainStormMediaGrouup.com

Buying media is like buying a new car, it's a negotiation. Unlike buying a car often you're at a disadvantage because you either don't know or don't understand the media world. Earlier I talked about the power of celebrity and that it can be created simply by being in the media, other than a spot or placement advertising. Unfortunately the same is true for the practice who's looking to buy print, radio, or TV time. Most think the ad reps have you at a disadvantage because they control the media time.

The first thing you have to understand about mass media time and space is that it's limited. Once the newspaper is printed, the radio or TV broadcast time is run, it can't be brought back, which is to say, once it's gone it's gone... it can't be resold. The reality is you as a customer, you have the control; you have the money and they want it. It's like Zig Ziglar used to say entering a prospect's home to sell his pots and pans, *"I have your pots and pans in my car and you have my money in your pocket, we need to exchange the two."*

In this chapter you're going to learn from a trusted resource of mine; an expert I have worked closely with for my erectile dysfunction clinic clients over the past several years. Jessica Jones is a media buying expert for all print, radio, and television. The following is a transcript of an interview I did with Jessica for a private coaching group. Jessica will give you a *"behind the curtain"* look at the mindset of the media ad reps and how to negotiate the best rates for your media, as well as give you a clear understanding of the power of each media and how to apply it in your marketing mix.

Let me take a moment to give you a little background on myself and how I got started in the media world.

Sure. It's a long story, but I started as a salesperson. So I very much know that side of things. And as a matter of fact, I ran a national radio company for about sixteen years. And as part of that, I was in charge of training all the salespeople in 26 different offices and overseeing sales and new business development. In addition, I placed radio on probably every radio station in the country plus Canada and Mexico.

We handled all the presidential campaigns. So no matter what the party, we were taking the call and putting that onto the radio. It was really interesting. We'd get a call from the republicans, "I need these twenty states." And then we'd get a call from the democrats, "I need these 30 states." And we had to do it all within a matter of hours because there's no direct response like the polls is what I say.

And so every day things were changing, and that's sort of what got me into this ability to sort of look at how things are working and figure out how to change it in the favor of the – of what we were looking for in terms of response. From that, I got a call – a lot of agencies would use me to – what we call white labeled. And they still white label me to do all of their planning and research and buying and all of that without a patient knowing that I'm there doing that part of the process.

And so that's how I started the company. I was just doing that and it's something that I really enjoyed. And then I got calls from people to work with them and it grew from there. And that's how I got introduced to the men's clinic. I had an agency who was working with them and they couldn't make the media work. So they came to me and that's how that all started. So I'm very grateful for that.

The rest is history. And just to give you an idea, we had a period of time for – it was about twelve weeks where I stopped working with them and they were checking – they tested two different agencies and response was down by 60 percent after that 12 weeks. And they came back to me and said, "Do you think we can turn it around?" And it was literally turned around within a week. And there's just a couple things, there's nuances to the way you place media that can make or break response, really. A lot of it is creative, but some of it is about where you're placing and all of those things.

So I guess one of the things I can talk about initially – you say you're speaking with media reps and they feel that their product is out of this – worth a lot more than you feel it is, I'd have to evaluate each individual package that you looked at, but one of the things I can tell you about sales reps today is they are miserable. They're so unhappy. And the way that they're being paid is really obscure. So for example, Clear Channel, they pay their media reps differently for – based on the length of a spot. So they might make more money selling you a 10 than a 60 or a 30 than a 60. They make more money selling you 7p to midnight spots than they do 6a to 10a spots on a percentage basis.

So it's so obscure how they're paid, but their incentive is not to put together the package that's going to work for you. Their incentive is to put together the package that's going to get them the commission and meet their quotas because they all have quotas on selling a different number of spots in each day part and a different number of spots in each length.

It's a combination of creative and placement. It's partly creative, and part in placing.

Working with the men's clinic we were placing print, radio and TV and we went to the lengths of testing what response was in mixing those. Some people prefer to read the paper, some prefer the radio and others

As for the strengths of each media it varies, but print you can definitely rely on still the older demographics to read the paper religiously. Senior citizens still get the paper and read it from cover to cover. Many of them. So that's something you can count on, but one of the things I say about the paper, and it's a different way of looking at the paper than it had been looked at before I took over that area, is just as there are different demographics reading the newspaper, there are different demographics that you can reach in the paper.

So somebody reading main news is pretty standard, but then, for example, I have a funeral client and for them I wouldn't be anywhere, other than the area pertinent. Nobody wants to open the Lifestyle section and read about a tombstone. But somebody who's recently had a death in the family or who is looking at the people who have passed in the past week, those people are starting to think about memorials or they're thinking about the end of life. So that's really the only section I'd be in for that patient.

So you can look at the different sections of a paper as though they're different segments of the population. And you can use your own mind to figure out and determine what section appeals to the different mindset. Does that make sense to everybody?

Dictating Your Print Media Placement

I will tell you, and this is a big deal, you do not need to sign a contract to get a discounted rate in the paper. You don't. You don't need a contract. It's always something that the papers push and it's quite antiquated and a lot of people who are old school believe that you need to do that to get the best rate, but you really don't. You just need to negotiate strongly and keep going back and keep going back and wear them down.

Another tactic I've – for somebody who really won't bend on the rates, just let them know when they come back to you, "Hey, are you going to place that?" "Oh, no I put the money into radio because it was more efficient." Always, always, ten out of ten times the rep will say, "Well, you should have let me know 'cause I could have negotiated further." "Well, I did let you know that I needed your best rate." And they will definitely negotiate better the next time around. So that's print.

Radio reaches the masses. There are plusses and minuses to every single one of the media. One of the things I will tell you is that a lot of people believe you have to be in drive time to make radio work. And drive time's considered 6:00 to 10:00 in the morning and 3:00 to 7:00 at night. Well, when it comes to response, I fervently disagree with that. In the morning, people are doing whatever it is they have to do to get out the door. So they're not as engaged with the listening as they are at other times of day. And the same thing with 3:00 to 7:00. They're winding up their workday or whatever they have to do and they're moving on to dinnertime.

So I have experienced that from 10:00 to 3:00 is really the best time to be advertising and getting an engaged listener who's going to actually hear the message to the extent that they'll be inspired to respond. And what they're saying about the best time is they're talking about numbers based on Arbitron ratings. And I've been to

Arbitron offices. It's not the most advanced system of tracking, but that said, yes, more people might be listening from 6:00 to 10:00, but we're not looking for that. What we're looking for is engaged listening, people actually listening, not having it on in the background or not doing a million other things while they're listening.

In midday, people are more willing to sit and listen to one station because they want that station. Whereas when you're in the car and you're moving, you just want something to keep you going, and that's why people tend to push the button more, I think, during that time of day.

People are much more likely to switch over the channel. There's no doubt that anyone in direct response will lament about him leaving the radio because he was a great person to capture response.

And then with TV, what I'll tell you, essentially, you really want to be in local news programming if you're looking for response. Everything else, there's just too many channels, too many choices, too fragmented of an audience. And by fragmented, I mean just divided up between all the people in the market. They have all of these choices and they're divided among all of them. But local news is local news and there's only so many choices for that. And people are actively watching it and not likely to turn the channel because they get associated and engaged with one local news team. They're connected to the personalities and they're not likely to change. They get their news from that source and they stay there for what they're looking for in the morning or in midday or evening.

And they're not as fragmented because there's so much fewer local choices when it comes to news. I'm not saying CNN doesn't work and other news channels. They do. ESPN for specific products. But if you want the best response for you, stick with local news.

Several of the Cable networks have "their own news" channels or news broadcasts. Are people connected to that as much as the local news or not? You will see the cable TV reps peddling their 'news' shows as the best thing since sliced bread.

However, the numbers are much, much lower when it comes to those news choices. A lot of times the Cable choices are somewhat of a spinoff of the local programming, but people still tune into the main parent station. And again, I'm not saying that there's areas of Cable that – areas of Cable can work, but local news is the first toe I'd dip in the water as it pertains to getting response from television.

That said, there's different purposes for getting your ad out there and there are unique instances, so it would just be on a specific patient basis that that might change.

For example, there's certain clients that are very – only a sports enthusiast might be interested in it. Well, for them, of course, I'd skip everything else and go right to ESPN.

It's really a matter of knowing your audience.

For a politician, I would be republican on Fox and right down the line on the Fox News Channel. I'd cover my bases everywhere on all of those news networks.

What About The 'Mix'?

Any time somebody sees an advertiser in more than one medium, it just reinforces that message and adds credibility and aids in response because it's reaching them on multiple touch points that they are engaged with and it gives them that sort of impetus to respond like, "Wow, I just –" they might even be able to pinpoint where they saw it.

One of the big fallacies is listening to people regarding response. People don't self-report where they heard your advertising or saw your advertising. It's really, really important that you track your response using something, other than your customers. So I recommend any cloud-based phone system to get phone numbers and a reporting. Yeah. Or hire somebody who can work on that with you. There's a lot of services that do a great job of tracking everything from your media spend to response by media outlet. And we can send Ron information if that'll help for another time.

But I highly recommend tracking response, not basing if off of your audience because people don't self-report. But what I will say is often times I will start with a certain media mix and then grow it from there. So I might start in a market with print, depending on the demo. But if I'm looking at an older audience, for example, I would start with print and radio and I'd watch the response there. And the important thing is watching the response and changing it literally every week.

So you go in and any source that's not pulling for you, move those dollars somewhere else so that you can really start getting a feel of what outlets are going to pull for you. And then you're starting a pattern of consistently shifting. And there is a time period where if you're not rotating enough ads, you can get what we call ad blindness where people just stop seeing your ad. And when that happens, you want to start rotating in new media.

So when that would happen, I might pull from one media and go into television in this scenario so that now I'm on radio and television. Or I might pull from radio and be heavier in print and television or it just depends on the scenario, but I do like to rotate the media. And then I also like to, once a new medium is rotated into the plan, sort of keep all of them going and just rotate how they're running so that those audiences aren't ever inundated with the message. And that's one way to avoid ad blindness.

Are you with me on that?

This all may sound difficult. It is! It's far more difficult than the media reps taking your money want it to be.

You'll find media reps are more interested in building you an ad or broadcast schedule; setting it and forgetting it... and taking your money to their bank and depositing it; rarely (if ever) interested in whether it worked for you or not. In reality they should be interested in it working for you because when that schedule runs out, guess who's going to be calling when that schedule expires? The ad rep. And what do you think that conversation's going to sound like? You know, because you've had it with your ad reps before.

I never place more than a week at a time, unless I have enough experience and the confidence to know that a station's going to consistently pull for me. And even then, I don't run on every station every week. I always move the media every week and I always base it on response. So it is complicated. So I watch response several times a day and on Thursday, typically – excuse me – I have enough information to make an educated decision about the following week.

So it might look to me like a newspaper is at an excessively-high cost per lead on a Thursday, but if I know that their ad isn't running again until Friday so that they only run on – ran on Monday and their next ad is Friday, I can get a sense of where they're going to end up at the end of the week. But I change everything every week. Every single media outlet based on response. So it's not easy. It is complicated.

Now, I buy a lot of media all over the country, but when you're buying your own media, no matter how big you or your budget is, remember something, it's their money. You can choose to say, "I only want to buy one week." Absolutely. And if the media outlet comes back to you and says, "Oh, well, we can't honor these rates, unless you book some sort of long-term plan", say, "Well, here's the situation. I'm placing my dollars based on what works. And if you can't honor these lower rates, I know for sure it's not going to work so I'm just going to put those dollars on the station that's willing to offer me the best rates."

You have complete control over where and how your money runs. You can say, "I want to run in X". You can say, "I only want to run for a week." You can say, "I only want to run on these three days of the week." It does take a lot of time and analysis to know what works, but if it's something that you want to take your time and do, you absolutely have control over how it works and you can certainly take the time to monitor and learn from that week what's working and what's not working.

When To Buy?

I don't buy evening – if there's a phone room that's open from 8:00 to 6:00 or 9:00 to 5:00, I would run in the noon news. And usually there's 4:00 news as well.

But you say you're not there to see, hear or read your ad because you're working. A lot of people are there though. And the benefit of that is the cost is usually lower. Remember, you might get more people in that 11:00 p.m. news hour, but they can't respond.

And at noon, you're paying for the people who are watching, so it's a lower price and you can hit them more than once in a day to try and mimic frequency. So what I'm saying is you can buy two spots in that half-hour program and now they've seen you twice. They might not respond the first time, but the second time they might start getting it. And then if the next day you're on there at the same time and you're going to get that same person again and at some point, they're going to be inspired to respond.

Of course the salesperson's going to try to push you into a package deal of some sort. You don't have – it's a really false belief out there that you've got to buy a bunch of spots to make things work. And that's one of the biggest false beliefs of the radio reps. And they really believe 'cause they've been fed this line, like, "Oh, you got to buy this many spots; otherwise, it's not going to work." That's just not true.

In fact, I had a patient recently looking at the advertising and say to me, "How can I be spending the same amount of money on this station in Jacksonville as I am on this station in New York?" Well, the answer to that is I'm buying to a budget and in New York with the number of people listening, I literally – there are stations where I buy five spots a week and that's it. It's about where they're placed that makes it work. If I bought seven spots on that station, their cost per lead would be out of whack and they'd be off the buy. If I bought four spots, probably the same thing. So I just happen to know that that station, the sweet spot is five to seven spots.

With this Clear Channel Station, I would say, again – it's funny 'cause I referred to them in the beginning. These reps are incentivized based on getting people to buy specific day parts, specific spot lengths, all of those things. It's not their fault. It's their company has a flawed commission structure. But as the patient, you've got to go in and just say, "I want to see the rates for every day part, I want the best rates you can offer." Even if you're only looking at Clear Channel, let them know, "I'm looking at every station in the market and I'm going to be a consistent advertiser, but that advertising's going to be based on response. I'm going to be measuring your results. Give me your best rates."

And then don't tell them what your plan is to buy. They're going to give you their rates for 6:00 to 10:00, 10:00 to 3:00, 3:00 to 7:00.

Don't let them know you're interested in 10:00 to 3:00. Let them give you rates for everything. And then negotiate as best you can and just place that buy for 10:00 to 3:00. And I'd recommend 10:00 to 3:00, Tuesday through Thursday, ten to fifteen spots. And that's it. One week. And you will know if it works 'cause you'll get phone calls or you won't. And that's where the creative comes in.

If you don't get all the phone calls you'd imagined, it might not be just the station. It might be a combination of the station and the message or it might be the message. And when it comes to the spot, it is very important everybody – in a print ad, always list your website, but in a radio ad, only give your phone number and make sure that you can give it at least three times at the end of the message. And not rush, call 888-888-8888. That's 888-888-8888. Call today, 888 – no. It's got to be slow so that people can get it in their memory or write it down if they have pen.

Ron's an expert at timing and cadence and message. Yes, for radio, you've got to use 60 seconds 'cause people don't have the visual and audio. They've only got the audio. So their mind is doing a lot of things while they're listening to that spot. It's got to be a good spot and it's got to be 60 seconds.

You want to hire a direct response writer, someone who's familiar with both direct response marketing and the media you want to use; someone who understands all aspects of message, creative and media.

The key in using print, radio or television, like any other media, is to test, test, test, measure and then test some more.

Jessica Jones is the president and founder of Rainstorm Media Group near Philadelphia, Pennsylvania. You can reach Jessica by email at jessica@rainstormmediagroup.com

Chapter 19

WHAT DO YOU DO NEXT?

The next step should be to take action. If you've struggled to get patient testimonials in your practice, or you've got testimonials and they're not the kind to attract your ideal patients then you definitely must take action right now.

What I've shared here is the information you can use to start getting powerful patient testimonials, and building a library to use in all your marketing and advertising. The contents in this book are either from my own experiences, those of my private clients, and other experts I work with. There are some problems though as you reach this point in the book and I want to take this time to solve these problems. You're probably excited about this now, but what you face with this information is the challenge of implementation.

You may think you have it. However, psychologists tell us you don't. Psychologists tell us we retain 83% of what we see, but forget 50% of it within 48 hours. You'll likely remember half of what you thought of as a result of what I shared here. And about 16 days from now, without having reread or refreshed yourself on this information, you won't likely even remember reading this book. You see, there's a problem with bridging the gap between this new information, new ideas and intentions to implementation; it's a huge gap. It works like my mom told me, *"in one ear and out the other"*.

Bridging the gap between new ideas, new information, new intensions to implementation doesn't happen with just thoughts, ideas or even dog eared pages and margin notes. It takes tools. I've really only scratched the surface on patient testimonials here. If you're truly serious about getting and using patient testimonials in your practice then you have 3 options right now:

1. Go it on your own with the information I've provided you here and figure out the nuances as you go

2. Delegate it to a team member and rely on their learning curve

3. Or put my team to work for you

"With integrity a lot of times you forget that your level is so much different than everyone else. You get lulled into believing that the world operates the same way that you do; the world's got a lot of integrity, but when you take a step outside of your world you find that's really not the case. So finding those high-integrity people like Ron can be difficult. And when you do you tend to want to grab a hold of them and run. That's why a guy like Dan Kennedy, another guru in marketing, is a client of Ron". It only makes sense that folks like us all migrate to people like Ron." Dr. James McAnally (CaseAcceptance.com)

"Social, peer and expert-authority proof; patient testimonials, stories – preferably emotions stories, patient human interest stories are all critically important element for practice marketing. What is grossly under-estimated is how much skill is required to obtain really good testimonials, to plan for strategically purposed testimonials, and specific to video, getting non-professionals to come across on camera as honest and authentic. I have worked for many days myself, in studios, and on locations, controlling filming of testimonials and peoples' stories for TV infomercials, sales videos/DVD's, and online video, and I have worked with top infomercial industry and Hollywood pros who specialize in filming such testimonials. Any monkey with an iPhone can shoot video these days, and that tempts. But the video is barely the half of it. Knowing who to shoot, what to shoot, and how to shoot, interacting with real patients not professional talent is not something just anybody can

do. Ron Sheets has made himself an absolute authority on patient testimonials and on the making and use of video of them. His understanding of how most testimonials fail to influence – what he calls 'survey testimonials' – is on target and itself worth reading this entire book. His explanation of the way dentists misunderstand what new patients are looking for, which must then sabotage their ability to get and use testimonials, is extremely perceptive. I have worked in marketing for health care professionals, practice and institutions for more than 30 years and I know for a fact he has his finger on something vitally important with this. It's a "secret", on page 19. I can attest to Ron's technical competence; I use him myself and for clients for various video projects. But as important, in this book, he has encapsulated what is required to get persuasive patient testimonials for use in any medium. Most doctors bluntly have no idea and therefor no good plan; they take what comes at random, and use what they get randomly. Ron's book drawn from his own experience working with dentists changes all that."
Dan Kennedy – strategic marketing advisor and direct-response consultant and copywriter. Author, 23 books, including *No B.S. Guide to Trust-Based Marketing* and *No B.S. Guide to Brand-Building by Direct-Response.* wwwNoBSBooks.com

If you're not sure how to get started then turn to the next page and learn about the entry level program I developed for dental practices. It will get you the kind of patient testimonials you really need, build a library of effective online reviews and you can then grow from there if you choose.

The Ultimate Patient Testimonial Machine
Put Patients In - Get Testimonials Out

Forget about trying to get someone on your staff to get this done. I've created a program specifically for independent dentists and dental practices to finally get patient testimonials captured.

This book is a summary of my 30+ years experience in asking for, capturing and implementing testimonials yet despite its 150+ pages, it really only scratches the surface on the subject. The nuances and skill required to properly get it done can't be captured in these pages.

The Ultimate Patient Testimonial Machine is the full complement of my system and team working for you; recruiting, asking for, and capturing your best patients' testimonials in video, audio, and/or print.

If you're tired of struggling with the "testimonial monster", then put my team and I to work for you. Go to www.UltimateTestimonialMachine.com to get started right now.

Once you enroll in the program you'll receive my complete guide on how to select the ideal patients as well as a 30-minute call with me to discuss how to implement the patient testimonials and reviews I get for you.

A special introductory opportunity is waiting for you. The normal monthly investment for this program is $697/month. Having purchased and read my book you can enter the program for only $297/month. Why would I do this? Because you need to have the right testimonials and reviews to attract the kind of patients you want, and do the kind of dentistry you love.

5 Reason You Want To Do This Right Now

1. You need patient testimonials
2. You've tried to get them on your own and you're frustrated by the process and you want it done
3. You're tired of hearing your staff tell you they don't have time to do
4. The testimonials you have now are terrible
5. You need a more powerful online reputation (reviews)

Go to: www.UltimateTestimonialMachine.com/book to get started right now.

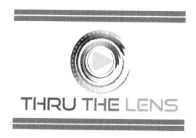

The television camera *captures* reality as it happens, it doesn't create it. My interview (or documentary) testimonial system captures patient testimonials as they are, in the patients own words. It's a form of marketing unscripted, but when I apply my editing skills to their words I'm able to turn those testimonials into powerfully persuasive ones for you.

Every day I'm talking with dental patients; extracting their stories and crafting them into powerful marketing messages for my private clients. My new publication, "Thru the Lens™", is replaced my monthly emailed newsletter *"Dental Marketing Update"* which focused on marketing in general. Thru the Lens™ will focus entirely on patient testimonials, online reviews and how to implement and leverage them in your dental practice. , and I will focus entirely on relationship marketing for independent and solo-doc dental practices.

As a member each month, you'll receive a brief, yet detailed case white paper in the mail that will give you a behind-the-scenes look into what I'm doing for my clients. You'll get to look over my shoulder each month as I craft a practice's patient experiences into powerful marketing. You'll be able to ethically steal my techniques and strategies and make them your own. Each month I'll go into greater detail on a case study with a patient's interview and/or dental specific work I'm doing with a private client.

Go to www.ThruTheLensOnline.com/book to subscribe now. The monthly membership is only $9.95/month and you'll receive my case studies in the mail each month. As a bonus for signing up you'll receive the audio CD of my interview with Jessica Jones free.

ABOUT THE AUTHOR

 Ron Sheetz is the founder of RJ Media Magic, Inc. He has become an expert in the application of television communication with more than 3 decades of experience. He has private clients in 37 different industries including the dental industry with private Dentists as clients across the U.S., Canada, England, Australia and Taiwan. He's been widely published in several dental specific books and thought leader's member publications. He's a highly sought after speaker on the subject of use and application of testimonials and relationship marketing. He produces 6 different publications each month and leads mastermind sessions on the subject. Ron is also a professional magician and certified hypnotherapist. He lives between 2 homes, primary residence in a suburb of Cleveland, Ohio and a second in Orlando, Florida with his wife Anne and 2 children, Brandon and Olivia.

39244082R00089

Made in the USA
San Bernardino, CA
18 June 2019